BIZARRE ENGLAND

BIZARRE
ENGLAND

DISCOVER THE CROQUET SECRETS & SURPRISES

BY DAVID LONG

Michael O'Mara

BIZARRE ENGLAND

DISCOVER THE COUNTRY'S SECRETS & SURPRISES

BY DAVID LONG

Michael O'Mara Books Limited

First published in Great Britain in 2015 by
Michael O'Mara Books Limited
9 Lion Yard
Tremadoc Road
London SW4 7NQ

A CIP catalogue record for this book is available from the British Library.

Papers used by Michael O'Mara Books Limited are natural, recyclable
products made from wood grown in sustainable forests. The
manufacturing processes conform to the environmental regulations of
the country of origin.

ISBN: 978-1-78243-376-7 in hardback print format
ISBN: 978-1-78243-377-4 in e-book format

1 2 3 4 5 6 7 8 9 10

Jacket illustration and design by Sara Mulvanny
Designed and typeset by K DESIGN, Winscombe, Somerset

Printed and bound by CPI Group (UK) Ltd, Croydon, CR0 4YY

www.mombooks.com

Contents

Introduction

The words 'English' and 'eccentric' go as well together as 'Great' and 'Britain', but in exploring the stranger aspects of English life one finds a lot more besides mad inventors and the usual countryside crackpots.

Who knew, for example, that Her Majesty the Queen uses her handbag to send coded messages to members of staff, or that she was once barred from an event at Windsor by a castle guard who mistook her for 'some old dear' who had lost her way?

Similarly none but the English would construct a set of gigantic concrete 'ears' on the south coast in the hope they could hear enemy aircraft taking off from France, or commission a special piece of music a thousand years long to be broadcast from the country's only inland lighthouse.

Everywhere one looks England throws up something comical, comically gruesome or just plain bizarre. Books bound in human skin, pubs where alcohol is never served, museums devoted to saltwater, cinema organs and sewing machines, and the famous Ugley Women's Institute – all life is here, it seems, and that's the way we like it.

From Boggy Bottom to Wetwang, from Crapstone to Splatt, there's barely a village or town in the country that doesn't have something which gets visitors scratching their heads – and that's very much the subject of this book. In it you'll find the questions that even most locals can't begin to answer. Stuff like: if the Royal Navy's HMS *Leigh* was more than a mile long, how come no one's ever heard of it? Why were inflatable lifejackets carried on Victorian trams? How long would it take an African elephant to walk from Scotland to Manchester, and why would it bother? And can it really be true that one of Jane Austen's eighteenth-century heroines said she preferred baseball to books?

1

Royal England

'I don't care what kind it is, just get me a beer.'

HRH The Duke of Edinburgh,
on being offered a glass of Italian wine

MORE Q.E. THAN Q.I.

🔔 In 1947, before Princess Elizabeth married, she was sent clothing coupons by hundreds of her father's loyal subjects. These were intended by the donors to be used to buy material for her dress, but sadly they had to be returned. Regulations concerning wartime rationing meant they were not transferable and that it was against the law to give them away.

🕊 In happier, more plentiful times at her 1953 Coronation, Queen Elizabeth II's robes used so much fabric and were so heavy that the Archbishop of Canterbury was asked to give Her Majesty a gentle shove to launch her along the nave of Westminster Abbey.

🕊 In 1991, the Queen was denied access to a private enclosure at the Royal Windsor Horse Show by security personnel. One of the guards apparently mistook her for 'some old dear who got lost'.

🕊 Her Majesty's Christmas message is presumed to be an annual fixture but is clearly optional, as in 1969 she gave it a miss. Apparently she believed the public had seen enough of her in a television documentary, *Royal Family*, broadcast earlier that year.

🕊 As well as a silver teapot, hot milk and water, Her Majesty's 7.30 a.m. wake-up tray includes a plate of biscuits for her beloved dogs. Since getting the first of these, Susan, in 1944, she has to date owned some thirty corgis. (Several are in fact dorgis, following an incident involving a dachshund owned by Princess Margaret.)

🕊 The Queen has long banked with Coutts & Co. The company installed a cash machine in Buckingham Palace, although it has never been suggested that this was for the sovereign's personal use.

🕊 Whilst Her Majesty's private diaries have not been published and are unlikely to be so, the entry for VE Day (8 May 1945) is known. It read: *Trafalgar Square, Piccadilly, Pall Mall, walked simply miles. Saw parents on balcony at 12.30am – ate, partied, bed 3am!*

The Queen doesn't require a number plate, but has one anyway – JGY 280, as far as we know a combination of no special significance – which George VI gave her on her eighteenth birthday. As an Auxiliary Territorial Services-trained wartime mechanic it is nice to think she might be quite handy with a spanner should any of her cars conk out.

THE LANGUAGE OF LUGGAGE

At official functions the Queen uses her handbag as a kind of semaphore. If she puts the handbag on a table, it alerts staff to the fact that she wishes to leave in five minutes' time. Transferring it from one arm to another during a conversation means she has had enough of talking with the same person.

The bag famously contains no money, although in reality the Queen does keep a crisply folded five- or ten-pound note for church collections. She also carries various good luck charms from her children. These include several miniature models of corgis and a photograph of the Duke of York on his return from the Falklands War.

Her Majesty even has her cars modified to accommodate the famous accessory. When a Daimler in which she had travelled between Buckingham Palace and Windsor Castle came up for auction, it was found to be fitted with an armrest designed to hold the handbag, and a hotline to Downing Street (this was disabled before the sale).

PUTTING A CAT AMONG THE PRINCES

A royal birth can make or break a nation, and historically new arrivals have not always been greeted by unalloyed joy.

Prince Edward (1470–83)

At the time of his birth, Edward's father had been deposed, and his wife, the commoner Elizabeth Woodville, was forced into hiding. Baptized 'like a poor man's child' and initially denied the title of Prince of Wales, on his father's death he was declared illegitimate and locked in the Tower of London. Murdered some time afterwards, as one of the two 'Princes in the Tower', the mystery of his death continues to fox even the most determined historians.

Prince Arthur (1486–1502)

As the son of Henry VII and the grandson of Edward IV, Arthur's arrival cemented the union of the squabbling houses of Tudor and York. His betrothal to Catherine of Aragon also offered the promise of an important political alliance with Spain, but then his early death meant we got his brother Henry instead: six wives, the destruction of the monasteries, and all the constitutional and religious upheaval anyone could want.

Prince Edward (1537–53)

Blessed with two daughters but desperate for a son, Henry VIII ordered a 2,000-gun salute at the news that his third wife had been delivered of a boy – but then lost his queen as the result of prolonged labour and an exceptionally difficult birth. The child fared only slightly better, succeeding to the throne as a nine-year-old but dying six years later.

Princess Charlotte (1766–1828)

George III's thirteen children produced fifty-six illegitimate offspring, but only one legitimate heir in Charlotte, the Princess Royal. Popular, and apparently well balanced for someone whose parents couldn't stand the sight of each other, she bore a son and heir but he was stillborn. Tragically, she died a few hours later, sparking an undignified race among her uncles to find themselves fertile wives in a bid to fill the gap.

Prince Augustus Frederick (1773–1843)

One of the uncles referred to above, George III's ninth child, married three times (twice to the same woman), but each time in secret and without seeking the permission of his father. As the law at the time required this, two marriages were annulled, and neither woman was ever recognized in court. The Prince was permitted to move into Kensington Palace, however, and was given the largest of the many spacious apartments. A lifelong bibliophile, he filled nearly a dozen rooms with an estimated 50,000 books (a tenth of which were copies of the Bible) and allowed his collection of exotic songbirds free rein to fly around the interior.

Princess Victoria (1819–1901)

With those uncles failing to come up with the goods, it seems extraordinary how much ill-feeling attended the birth of Victoria, especially given how well she turned out in the end. Her father declared the new arrival was more of 'a Hercules than a pocket Venus'. Her mother resented her deeply, after being forced to race back from Germany to ensure the baby was born on English soil. George III was too mad to care, and the Prince Regent was so upset at losing his daughter that he couldn't think of anything nice to say.

As for the remaining uncles, they were doubtless hacked off that they had lost the race to father a sovereign, and the public wasn't overjoyed either. For one thing the name Victoria was still unknown in this country, leading everyone to assume it was probably French. This was a mistake, and so soon after the Napoleonic Wars it was one the Royal Family could ill afford. Senior politicians prevailed on her mother to change it, but she refused, and so with a name no one liked and few could understand, Victoria acceded to the throne as an eighteen-year-old girl.

INK'S ROYAL LINKS

Scotland's Royal Military Tattoo may be more famous, but only because no one has been allowed to see English royalty's skin tattoos.

Like many a sailor, the future George V fancied a little epidermal modification. When his ship HMS *Bacchante* travelled to Japan in 1881, and before calling on the Emperor (to present him with a couple of wallabies, as you do), the prince found a design that he liked enough to indelibly ink a blue and red dragon onto the royal arm.

It's a fair bet that his grandmother Victoria would not have been amused, but his father was unable to complain, for he too had been tattooed. Nearly twenty years earlier, as Prince of Wales, Edward VII had had a Jerusalem Cross tattooed onto his arm while visiting the Holy Land. When he came to the throne he took care to ensure that it was never seen again, and George V did likewise a few years later.

ROYAL NICKNAMES

Alfred probably never complained about being called great, nor Athelstan glorious, but not every English sovereign has been blessed with the nickname he – or she – might have chosen.

Anne ....Brandy Nan
Edward VII ....Tum Tum
Elizabeth II.................Brenda
Aethelred II................The Unready
George I.......................Turnip Head
George III ....Farmer George
George IV....................The Prince of Whales
George V ....Grandpa England
Harold I.......................Harefoot
Henry VIII.................Bluff King Hal
James I.........................The Wisest Fool in Christendom
John ....Softsword
Matilda........................Empress Maud
Mary I ....Bloody Mary
Richard III ....Crookback
Stephen........................The Irresolute
Victoria ....Grandmother of Europe
William I.....................The Bastard
William II ....Rufus (i.e. Ginger)
William IV ....The Royal Tar

UNUSUAL ROYAL FIRSTS

- Elizabeth I was the first monarch to have her own flushing loo, known as Ajax. This novel throne was designed for her by her godson Sir John Harington, whom she had earlier banned from court for telling smutty stories.

- George IV was the first royal to have employed prizefighters as bouncers at his coronation although, to be fair, this hasn't become a royal habit. Above all, they were required to prevent his estranged wife from gaining entry to Westminster Abbey.

- Henry VIII was the first royal to double his waistline during his reign. In a typical year, he and his court would consume 1,200 oxen, more than 8,000 sheep, 2,300 deer, 750 calves, nearly 2,000 pigs, more than 50 wild boar and 4.8 million pints of ale, making the 132 cm waist not that much of a surprise.

- Effete and something of a fop, Richard II was the first royal to use a handkerchief. Indeed, he is credited with the invention of what official documents of the time referred to as 'little pieces for the King to wipe and clean his nose'.

- A 1324 statute means that any whale or sturgeon which washes up on the shore belongs to the Crown, but Prince Charles is the first royal to have ridden on the back of one.

- No member of the Royal Family had ever been to Australia until 1867 when Queen Victoria's son Prince Alfred paid a visit during his time in the Royal Navy. He was joyfully received, but in 1868, when he returned after a short jaunt, a man who had only recently been discharged from a lunatic asylum shot him in the back.

Alfred survived and Henry James O'Farrell was hanged shortly afterwards.

🍂 George's father, Edward VII, was the first king to wear a fireman's uniform. He so much enjoyed watching buildings on fire that he had his own made so that he could join in the fun without being identified.

🍂 Princess Anne was the first royal to qualify for a Heavy Goods Vehicle licence, and the first to be caught speeding – in a plastic-bodied Reliant Scimitar. (Aged nought, she became the one millionth member of the Automobile Association, and its first baby.)

HENRY 2.5

Everyone knows England has had eight King Henries. In fact there was a ninth, between Henry II and Henry III.

The second of five sons born to Henry II and Eleanor of Aquitaine (and the first to survive infancy) this one was crowned King of England during his father's lifetime as well as being made Duke of Normandy and Count of Anjou and Maine. Doing it this way was a French habit which otherwise didn't catch on in England, but whilst known during his lifetime as Henry the Young King (1155–83) he died of dysentery before acceding to the throne. As he'd just finished ransacking various monasteries in an attempt to raise funds to fight his father this early demise may have been no bad thing.

2

Natural England

'This blessed plot, this earth, this realm, this England.'

John of Gaunt, from *The Tragedy of King Richard II*
(1623) by William Shakespeare

РОЗА ЛЮБЫМ ДРУГИМ ИМЕНЕМ[1]

There is no flower more English than an English rose,
yet the oldest known depiction of the flower appears on a
Siberian grave dating back to 4000 BC.

ை ை ை

In Biblical times roses were found only in the Middle and
Far East, where they were cultivated not only for their
beauty and scent but for their oil, which was a valuable
natural preservative. Even when finally they arrived in
Europe, courtesy of the Crusaders, they were grown only
by monks for medicinal use and to make jam.

---

[1] A rose by any other name

The rose's migration from medicine to much-loved garden decoration didn't occur until the nineteenth century. This was down to Joséphine de Beauharnais, Empress of France. She had Napoleon search all seized ships for roses to feed her passion, and amassed as many as 250 different varieties.

ᘓᕲ ᘓᕲ ᘓᕲ

The rose's variety is undoubtedly a large part of its appeal. With something to suit every garden and every gardener, there are old roses, wild roses, shrub, climbing and rambler roses, standard and miniature roses, bushes and rugosa roses, yes, even English roses, Hybrid Teas and Floribunda, available in virtually every colour under the sun.

(Although the latter fact didn't sway Winston Churchill's children in 1958. Wishing to commemorate their parents' fiftieth wedding anniversary, the four got together to create a stunning Golden Rose Walk at Chartwell in Kent using only yellow ones – albeit in an incredible thirty-two different shades.)

ᘓᕲ ᘓᕲ ᘓᕲ

With names ranging from Agnes to Zigeunerknabe, it's possible to buy a Duke of Edinburgh rose, a Dorothy Perkins rose, a *Brother Cadfael* rose, a James Mason rose, even a *Radio Times* rose. Splash out on a José Carreras rose, a lovely tight white bloom with a creamy ivory centre, and 50p from each plant goes to support the opera star's International Leukaemia Foundation.

ᘓᕲ ᘓᕲ ᘓᕲ

One commercial grower, David Austin Roses in the Midlands, boasts more than 900 different varieties, but most thrilling is the family-owned Cants of Colchester, which has been in business since 1765. The earliest document in the company's archive, dated 1791, records a break-in by two thieves who absconded with four ducks, thirty nectarines and twelve peaches.

PETS FOR UKIP: ENGLAND'S ILLEGAL ALIENS

At Europe's busiest airport a dedicated facility called the Heathrow Animal Reception Centre (HARC) receives and cares for more than 80 million animals each year. These include 45 million invertebrates, 7 million live eggs, 28 million fish and around 13,000 cats and dogs. Carriers using the airport have also transported lions, rhinos, racehorses and sharks – and Lola the Hippo, who was given a shower just before her 2012 flight to ensure maximum comfort.

But not all new arrivals go through the correct channels and over the years many alien species have slipped into the countryside unobserved.

കൗ കൗ കൗ

Chester Zoo's first capybara, for example, was a gift from the second Duke of Westminster in the 1930s. The animal had been given to His Grace, at the time possibly the richest man in Europe, who built a house for it on an island on the lake at his Cheshire estate. It kept escaping because, having never seen one before, none of the Duke's servants realized that the giant South American rodent was amphibious.

After one getaway too many, the Duke did the sensible thing and placed it in the care of experts. Alas, similarly inappropriate pets are all too often released into the wild, often with disastrous results.

കൗ കൗ കൗ

On the Derbyshire–Nottinghamshire border, terrapins the size of dinner plates have been seen swimming in the Erewash Canal. These are assumed to have been bought as tiny juveniles during the 1990s craze for *Teenage Mutant Ninja Turtles*, only to be abandoned once their voracious appetite for dragonflies, fish, frogspawn – and even coots and small ducks – began to exceed expectations.

Slightly smaller specimens have been fished out of the Ashby Canal on the Leicestershire–Derbyshire border, but no one thinks it will be possible to catch all the wild terrapins.

As the creatures live for up to forty years, naturalists say the best hope is that the damp Midlands climate remains too cold for them to breed.

の の の

Further south, Aesculapian snakes, natives of southern and central Europe, have been found swimming in our waterways. Newspaper reports briefly waxed hysterical, suggesting that monster varieties would soon start strangling local cats and dogs but experts denied this, claiming that the snakes would be too shy to cause a real nuisance and would limit their threats to the local rat population.

の の の

In 2009, a young skunk was recovered from the Forest of Dean, prompting rumours that the North American natives were breeding. Appealing photographs of other wild skunks followed and it emerged that, providing their infamous scent glands were removed, they made jolly good pets. This operation was eventually declared illegal, rendering any new offspring unsuitable for sale as domestic companions. Consequently, as expert and omnivorous scavengers, skunks have started competing with badgers in the race to find birds' eggs and young birds.

The Forest of Dean is also home to hundreds of wild boar, highly destructive creatures which, despite the name, are technically farm animals bred like sheep and cows for the production of meat. Those now running free are thought to have been illegally released by animal rights activists, and as many as 400 are at risk of culling. This follows a number of attacks on dogs walking in the area by big pigs weighing up to 150 kg.

の の の

Famed for its thick, luxurious coat, the American mink looks cute but is another dangerous predator. Liberated from fur farms by well-meaning vegetarians, in Norfolk they have caused terrible damage to local populations of pheasant, partridge, moorhen, ducks and, perhaps worst of all, water voles (lovely Ratty, to those who enjoyed *The Wind in the Willows*). Mink frequently kill more than they eat, and treat their supposedly secure pens like hotels.

ও ও ও

Kent's yellow-tailed scorpions sound even worse but happily they are nowhere near as dangerous as the name would suggest. Many have been spotted around Sheerness Docks, presumably after a breeding pair or a fertile female somehow sneaked through Customs.

ও ও ও

As if Britain's poor honey bees didn't have enough to contend with, what with the varroa mite and the deadly mystery of Colony Collapse Disorder, a new species of Asian hornet was accidentally released in France and is now thought likely to be on its way. Preferring to travel in shipping containers rather than the arduous cross-Channel flight, the hornets like honey a lot and – unlike wasps – will happily attack bees in their hives in order to secure a supply.

ও ও ও

Finally, molluscs. The stripy zebra mussel has been here for more than a century and, as well as trashing native species, has been shown to damage harbours, ships and boats, and even water treatment and power plants which become clogged by the larvae. One English water authority claims to be spending £500,000 a year dealing with the menace.

Now the zebra mussel has been joined by the Ponto-Caspian quagga, named after a half-striped and now sadly extinct relative of the famous African quadruped. The quagga mussel is native to the Black and Caspian seas but travels further afield by attaching itself to ships' hulls. Once bedded down in a new home, it filters water to feed itself and does this so efficiently (at up to 50 litres an hour) that rival species simply starve to death.

SLOW AND STEADY . . .

In the summer of 2014 it was announced that Tommy the tortoise, England's oldest family pet, was to celebrate his 116th birthday.

Having survived two World Wars and lived to see six monarchs seated on the throne – Victoria, Edward VII and VIII, George V and VI and our own Queen – Tommy was still living with the same family in suburban Surrey. His present carer, Sheila Floras, is granddaughter of the original owner.

Tommy is actually female, although no one realized this for nearly a hundred years, until one morning she laid several eggs. In 1909 she cost £1 to buy, which was quite a handsome sum when she was sold, as a ten-year-old, at Croydon market. On the other hand, you get what you pay for, and in all that time none of her owners has ever had to pay to see the vet.

. . . WINS THE RACE

England, in fact, has something of a track record with tortoises. In the grounds of Powderham Castle in Devon is the grave of Timothy (1839–2004), who served as a Royal Navy mascot after being liberated from a Portuguese privateer in the mid-1850s. Timothy too was an unidentified female, the art of tortoise-sexing being something of a mystery to the Victorians.

However, and notwithstanding Timothy's great age, the country's most remarkable example of the breed must be Rotumah, a Galapagos giant found living in the grounds of an Australian lunatic asylum and brought back to Tring by the second Baron Rothschild.

A reluctant banker but talented and determined amateur zoologist, as a young man Lionel Walter Rothschild spent the equivalent of £7 million buying insect specimens but then had to sell 295,000 stuffed birds to pay off a (reputedly titled) female blackmailer. He never married, lived with his mother for all but three years of his life, and used to ride Rotumah whilst dangling a lettuce leaf in front of his face in a bid to squeeze out an extra few yards-per-hour. There are photographs to prove this, together with another of the six-foot-three-inch peer arriving at Buckingham Palace in a carriage pulled by a team of zebra.

A sub-species of giraffe (*Giraffa camelopardis rothschildi*) was named after Lord Rothschild, together with 153 insects, 58 birds, 17 mammals, 3 fish, 3 spiders, 2 reptiles, a millipede and a type of worm. When he died, his collection of preserved animals – by far the world's largest and at its peak, numbering many million – was bequeathed to the British Museum.

BEWARE THE ERMINTRUDER

Ordinarily, one might not place cows anywhere on a list of England's most dangerous animals, let alone the top. But the figures say otherwise.

In ten years to 2011, bulls killed 15 members of the public, seriously injuring 77 and leaving another 82 requiring treatment. Over the same period, cows were responsible for

17 deaths while injuring 362 people and sending a similar number to Accident & Emergency departments.

No other animal comes close. Not wild boar, not red deer which can grow to almost 3 metres in height, not even the worst attack dog with the worst owner on the worst sink estate in the worst part of the most depressed town in the whole of England. Even the adder, Britain's only venomous snake, has killed a mere fourteen people since 1876 – and none at all in the last forty years.

TREES A CROWD

There's nothing to compare with a fine English oak but one of the peculiarities of these arboreal icons is that as they age they become squatter rather than taller. Exceptionally old specimens, such as the celebrated Quarry Oak at Croft Castle in Herefordshire – thought to have been a sapling around the time William the Conqueror stepped ashore – risk suffocating as they compete for sunlight with nearby trees which are taller and much younger.

England's most voluminous tree is also to be found at Croft, a sessile oak comprising an incredible 3,800 cubic feet of wood making it Britain's largest living *thing*. Also of note are the neighbouring chestnut trees, grown from nuts recovered from ships of the Spanish Armada. One hopes it is only coincidence that Croft is the first castle in England to be heated by wood-chip boiler.

Perhaps the country's rarest tree is the Audley End oak (*Quercus audleyensis*) in Essex. This was planted in 1772 at the Jacobean estate of that name, since when every attempt to grow or graft from it has failed.

DRESSING FOR AN ENGLISH SUMMER

The English have been talking about the weather for centuries, and keeping records for almost as long, which shows that while it is reliably unreliable it can also occasionally throw up a few surprises.

Hottest ever day: 38.5°C
Faversham, Kent
10 August 2003

Coldest ever day: −26.1°C
Newport, Shropshire
10 January 1982

Coldest spell: 0°C
Kew, Surrey
17–25 January 1963

Largest hailstone: 190 g
Horsham, Sussex
5 September 1958

Wettest place: 3,400 mm average annual rainfall
Seathwaite, Borrowdale (Cumbria)
1971–2000

Worst deluge: 378 mm rainfall
Seathwaite, Borrowdale, Cumbria
34 hours, November 2009

Worst storm:15,000 dead
Southern England
24 November 1703

Worst avalanche: Eight dead
Lewes, East Sussex
27 December 1836

Worst flood: 307 dead
Eastern Counties
31 January 1953

Worst heatwave: *c.* 2,000 dead
Nationwide
3–13 August 2003

Worst mid-summer shower: 170 mm rainfall
London
2 hours, 14 August 1975

Still in Essex, the Yeldham Great Oak is one of many claimants to the title of England's oldest oak, despite being so obviously dead. Trees from the area were used for shipbuilding from the tenth century onwards, and the Yeldham appears on the first large-scale map of the county, published in 1777. By 1863 it was thought necessary to plant a new one to celebrate the marriage of the Prince of Wales and Alexandra of Denmark, and the old iron-bound hulk was finally preserved for posterity by public subscription in 1949.

∽ ∽ ∽

Vandalism can occasionally come good. Whilst billeted on the 5,000-acre Ashridge estate in Hertfordshire (another National Trust property) in the 1940s, American servicemen carved the initials of their home states into a mature beech tree. Fortunately, the tree withstood its decorations, and today stands as both a living monument and a moving war memorial.

∽ ∽ ∽

Arguably England's most famous tree is *the* apple tree in the garden of Woolsthorpe Manor, Isaac Newton's childhood home in Lincolnshire. Around 350 years old and still producing apples (which are often filched by visitors), the tree collapsed in the mid-nineteenth century – a victim of Newton's newfangled gravity – before beginning to grow upright once more.

∽ ∽ ∽

At Ankerwyke on the Berkshire–Surrey border, in the ruins of an ancient priory, the split wreckage of a tree some 8 metres wide is almost certainly England's oldest. The ragged yew is known to be at least 1,400 years old, and possibly a thousand years older than that. Legend has it that it marks the spot where Henry VIII and Anne Boleyn would meet to fool around; more certain is that the opposite bank of the Thames is where his predecessor King John was prevailed upon to put his seal to Magna Carta.

Borrowdale in Cumbria was home to a quartet of yews mentioned in Wordsworth's *Yew-Trees* (1803). One blew down during a storm in 1883 but another is now large enough for four or five people to crowd into the hollow trunk. A third at Lorton gave shelter to John Wesley, the Methodist founder, when he travelled north to preach.

കൈ കൈ കൈ

England's official thickest tree is nicknamed 'Majesty', a pedunculate oak 13 feet in diameter. It grows in Fredville Park, a privately owned estate near Dover, Kent.

കൈ കൈ കൈ

The pollution-resistant plane tree (*Platanus x acerifolia*) is most closely associated with the sooty streets of London, but the largest example in England – its branches spreading over more than 1,500 square metres – is in the grounds of Hampshire's twelfth-century Mottisfont Abbey.

കൈ കൈ കൈ

A very old pollarded sycamore at Tolpuddle in Dorset provided shelter for six aggrieved farm labourers who, too broke in 1834 to feed their families, swore a secret oath thus establishing what in effect amounted to an illegal trade union. For their trouble, the so-called Tolpuddle Martyrs were transported to Australia until a petition of more than 800,000 signatures and several protest marches eventually persuaded the authorities to reverse their sentences. At that time the *Acer pseudoplatanus* would already have been a 150 years old.

3

Visitor's England

'I can't think of anything that excites a greater sense of childlike wonder than to be in a country where you are ignorant of almost everything.'

Bill Bryson, author

THE HEART OF ENGLAND

Admittedly a minor matter among those debated during 2014's Scottish 'neverendum', a discussion was had about the whereabouts of the precise centre of the United Kingdom. Trivial, perhaps, but important for any traveller hoping to find the heart of a country.

The usual answer is Haltwhistle in Northumberland. It has a welcome sign reading 'Welcome to the Centre of Britain', a Centre of Britain hotel, a Centre of Britain gallery, even a Centre of Britain launderette. But the evidence is contentious to say the least, and relies on a claim that Haltwhistle lies equidistant from the respective centres of England, Scotland, Wales and Northern Ireland.

This may be correct if one accepts that the four centres are Meriden, the Forest of Atholl, Carno and Pomeroy – but many don't. Taking just the English example, it is easy to see why this is. There are, it seems, many different ways of determining the centre of such an irregularly shaped mass as a country and interested parties simply pick the one that suits them best.

Meriden near Coventry has made the claim longer than anyone else, and has an obelisk which locals insist marks the geographical centre of England. This is actually a memorial to cyclists killed in the Great War, although it may have been erected at the village centre.

Morton in Derbyshire is one of Meriden's many convincing rivals. It lies midway along England's longest north–south axis and is halfway between the East Coast and the Welsh border – which certainly sounds like the centre.

But then there's Lindley Hall Farm near Fenny Drayton in Leicestershire. It has a plaque describing it as England's centroid, the point at which a cardboard cut-out of England would balance perfectly on the tip of a pencil. This sounds silly except that the complex maths for the claim were carried out by the cartographers at Ordnance Survey.

Mind you, Church Flatts Farm in the delightful-sounding Derbyshire village of Coton in the Elms also claims to have the backing of Ordnance Survey. It has been officially declared as the point in England which is farthest from the sea, meaning the most inland spot, and presumably the most central.

Finally, we have the place known only by its coordinates: 52.66°N 1.85°W. The precise though somewhat anonymous map reference marks a spot somewhere between Hammerwich and Wall in Staffordshire. This is said to be furthest from the high tide marks, another unimpeachable, if arcane, measure.

ENGLAND'S MOST SINGLE-MINDED MUSEUMS

Turkey has a museum of hair, America one showing nothing but salt and pepper shakers, Croatia another celebrating broken relationships, and in Japan there's one devoted to instant ramen noodles. England too boasts more than its fair share of strangely specific collections. All are open to the public, but rarely seven days a week, so do check before travelling.

Anaesthetics:	Portland Place, London
Balloons:	Southampton, Hampshire
Bottles:	Elsecar, Yorkshire
Brine:	Droitwich Spa, Worcestershire
Chairs:	High Wycombe, Buckinghamshire
Cinema Organs:	St Albans, Hertfordshire
Cuckoo Clocks:	Tabley, Cheshire
Fans:	Greenwich, London
Gas:	Leicester
Glass:	Sunderland
Laurel & Hardy:	Ulverston, Cumbria
Lawnmowers:	Southport, Lancashire
Locks & Keys:	Willenhall, West Midlands
Mental Health:	Wakefield, Yorkshire
Mustard:	Norwich, Norfolk
Needles:	Redditch, Worcestershire
Pedal Cycles:	Harlow, Essex
Pencils:	Keswick, Cumbria
Penny-Farthings:	Knutsford, Cheshire
Prams:	Pailton, Rugby, Warwickshire

Radios: .... Ryde, Isle of Wight

Sewing Machines: ...... Balham, London

Shoes: .... Street, Somerset

Teapots: .... Maidstone, Kent

Telephones: .... Milton Keynes, Buckinghamshire

Tiling: .... Ironbridge, Shropshire

Wine: .... Alfriston, Sussex

Witchcraft: .... Boscastle, Cornwall

BE AMAZED

- Hampton Court Palace Maze, England's oldest, was planted in the late 1600s for King William III of Orange. Covering just a third of an acre it contains a staggering half a mile of twisting paths.

- The Marquess of Bath's maze at Longleat, Wiltshire, comprises more than 16,000 yew trees and is unusual in that six raised bridges at strategic points enable anyone lost to view it from above.

- Another 3-D offering is Ragley Hall Maze in Warwickshire, constructed on two levels with wooden platforms and stairways doubling your chances of getting lost.

- York Maze, a temporary structure made up of a million living maize plants, is larger still – ten times the size of a football pitch – and the design varies from year to year to ensure no one can cheat by memorizing the layout.

- The Minotaur Maze in the grounds of Northumberland's Kielder Castle is built from natural basalt gabions and recycled glass with a dazzling glass chamber at its centre for anyone able to find their way through.

- Hever Castle Water Maze in Kent has low hedges, making it easy to navigate. The trick is to avoid being drenched by hidden jets of water and tilting tiles which boobytrap the path to the centre.

- Still in Kent, Leeds Castle Maze combines circles in a square with a castle at the centre beneath which a fabulous grotto and an underground tunnel offer an escape route for anyone too confused to find their way out.

- Around 14,000 beech trees and two miles of paths make Noah's Ark Maze at Wraxall near Bristol Europe's longest. The name describes the shape, and successful navigation requires questions to be answered, as well as the usual skills.

PRIVATE PARTS

From Bedlam in North Yorkshire via Nottinghamshire's Rhodesia to Shropshire's Ruyton-XI-Towns – and let's not forget Essex and its infamous Ugley Women's Institute – a list of villages with silly names could easily fill a book, so to keep it brief these are just the slightly rude ones:

Bachelors Bump .... East Sussex

Backside Lane .... Doncaster

Bell End .... Worcestershire

Bitchfield .... Lincolnshire

Boggy Bottom .... Hertfordshire

Bottoms Fold .... Lancashire

Brown Willy .... Cornwall

Claggy Bottom .... Hertfordshire

Cockintake .... Staffordshire

Cockplay .... Northumberland

Cockup .... Cumbria

Crapstone .... Devon

Crotch Crescent .... Oxford

Devil's Lapful .... Northumberland

Dicks Mount .... Suffolk

Faggot .... Northumberland

Fanny Barks .... Durham

Fanny Hands Lane ..... Lincolnshire

Jolly's Bottom .... Cornwall

Juggs Close .... East Sussex

Lickey End .... Worcestershire

Lower Swell .... Gloucestershire

Nether Wallop .... Hampshire

Nob End .... South Lancashire

Nork Rise .... Surrey

North Piddle .... Worcestershire

Old Sodbury .... Gloucestershire

Old Sodom Lane .... Wiltshire

Pant .... Shropshire

Penistone .... Yorkshire

Prickwillow .... Cambridgeshire

Scratchy Bottom .... Dorset

Shitterton .... Dorset

Spanker Lane .... Derbyshire

Splatt .... Cornwall

Swell .... Somerset

Titty Hill .... Sussex

Titty Ho .... Northamptonshire

Weedon Lois .... Northampton

Wetwang .... Yorkshire

Wham Bottom Lane ... Lancashire

Wideopen .... Newcastle

Willey .... Warwickshire

STONEHENGE'S NOT SO SPLENDID ISOLATION

After more than 5,000 years we know more or less how England's most famous prehistoric monument was built, but still not why it was built. Recently the mystery deepened when it was revealed that one of its most striking features – that fabulous remote location – is a relatively modern thing.

During four years of sophisticated geophysical surveys, researchers from the University of Birmingham discovered a further seventeen shrines in the area. This suggests that today's isolated stone circle originally formed part of a complex of similar structures, one of which would have covered nearly five square miles and dwarfed what we see today.

These included what archaeologists are calling 'Super Henge', said to be nearly a mile wide, and a building more than 30 metres in length. The latter was already a thousand years old before the construction of Stonehenge even began, and may have been used for excarnation, the grisly process by which early man stripped the flesh from the bones of the dead.

ALL THE ZOOS THAT'S FIT TO PRINT

- The earliest known use of the word 'zoo', an abbreviation of zoological garden, was in 1847 and referred to Clifton Zoo. Now called Bristol Zoo, and the world's oldest provincial establishment of this kind, it bred the first chimpanzee in Europe (1934) and Britain's first black rhino (1958).

- Chester Zoo, the most popular animal attraction in the country, built some of its original animal enclosures using materials recycled from wartime pillboxes and anti-tank traps.

- Manchester's Belle Vue, England's first privately financed zoo, already kept kangaroos, rhinos, lions and bears in the 1850s. Plans to acquire an elephant ran into trouble when the £680 animal charged the train, causing such great damage that it was decided to walk the animal down from Scotland. The journey took ten days.

- Cotswold Wildlife Park is the only zoo in Europe to have successfully bred wolverines.

- Howletts in Kent was established by John Aspinall using profits from a series of illegal gambling houses he ran in Mayfair in the 1950s.

- Built in the grounds of a ruined eleventh-century castle, Dudley Zoo is as famous for its architecture as for its inhabitants. Twelve buildings are listed, half of them Grade II* (two star), as fine examples of thirties Modernism designed by the Jewish emigré Berthold Lubetkin (1901–90).

- Woburn Safari Park was created by the thirteenth Duke of Bedford as a means of paying off double-death duties levied by a socialist government. Visitors could pay extra to have their photograph taken with His Grace, or be photographed with a cardboard cut-out of him free of charge.

- When it opened in the mid-sixties, Longleat, the brainchild of circus owner Jimmy Chipperfield, offered the only drive-through safari anywhere outside Africa.

- Windsor Safari Park (now Legoland) featured in the horror movie *The Omen* (1976), when a family of crazed baboons attacked a car containing Lee Remick. The warden who helped to film the scene was killed by a lion the following day, fuelling rumours that the film was cursed.

- During the Blitz, Whipsnade Zoo in Bedfordshire was considered a safe place to evacuate animals from London Zoo. Unfortunately, it was bombed more than forty times, literally scaring one giraffe to death. Several animals were then returned to London on the grounds that this might boost morale (among the humans).

FAWLTY ADVICE

Concerned perhaps that too many hoteliers may look upon the hotelier created by John Cleese as a role model, VisitBritain, the taxpayer-funded body charged with enhancing England's appeal to foreign visitors, recently issued detailed guidelines for anyone involved in the country's booming tourist trade. Tips included useful advice about visitors, for example:

Canadians hate to be mistaken for Americans.

Indians don't like it when we mock their accents, and like to change their minds frequently.

Australians are trying to be friendly not rude when they call us 'Poms'.

Belgians don't like to discuss money, or the fact that their country has two official languages.

Guests from Hong Kong may take fright if offered a four-poster bed or asked to sleep in an historic country house hotel.

Japanese visitors take offence if they are shouted at, and don't enjoy being told 'No'.

Like Austrians, Germans don't mean to be 'rude and aggressive' merely 'straightforward and demanding'.

Russians prefer rooms with high ceilings and large doors.

The French don't like us to smile at them or to maintain eye contact for too long.

COY EXHIBITIONISM

Sometimes deliberately hidden, many of England's most intriguing artworks take some tracking down. Coming across this sort of thing in the middle of nowhere can be bizarre but is a welcome antidote to many of the better-known galleries where during big shows visitor numbers can be so high that it can be impossible to see some of the exhibits.

- A small herd of cows made from recycled bits of diggers are visible to cyclists making their way from Consett to Sunderland.

- All Saints' Church at Tudeley in Kent contains twelve glass panels by Marc Chagall. These were commissioned in the late-1960s by Sir Harry d'Avigdor Goldsmid Bt as a memorial for his daughter who drowned.

- Bob Budd's *Eating for England*, a gigantic metal spoon, is situated in the middle of a field a few miles south of Cramlington, Northumberland.

- In Middlesbrough, a series of oversized tools by Andrew Mckeown have been used to enliven local industrial estates.

- More pagan than Christian, the Zennor Mermaid is carved on the end of a pew at St Senara's Church in the Cornish village of that name.

- *Silvas Capitalis* in the Kielder Forest, a giant head made from 3,000 pieces of timber, offers not just shelter – it is large enough for several to enter – but a great view through the eye-sockets.

- In Kendal's Quaker Meeting House in Cumbria nearly eighty intricate tapestries tell the story of Quaker history from its foundation to the present day. They were created by more than 4,000 individual Quakers over fifteen years.

- Carved out of the wall of Tout Quarry in Portland, *Still Falling* by Antony Gormley forms part of the Dorset Sculpture Trail, but is easy to miss.

- Situated high above the finest grousemoor in England, *Clougha Pike* in Lancashire was commissioned from Andy Goldsworthy by the Duchess of Westminster and stands sentinel like three drystone sentry boxes.

- An ancient manmade cave in Royston, Hertfordshire, contains a series of bizarre Christian and pre-Christian images carved into the chalk walls. Clearly medieval, these include an erotic Sheela-na-gig, as well as depictions of several saints including Catherine of Alexandria, George and Christopher.

- Thirty-four metres high and nearly half a kilometre in length, the largest naked female sculpture in the world also lies near Cramlington. Seven years in the planning, it was created by Charles Jencks using waste from an open-cast mine.

4

Transporting England

I will pack, and take a train,
And get me to England once again!
For England's the one land, I know,
Where men with Splendid Hearts may go.

Rupert Brooke (1887–1915), poet

BIZARRE BEGINNINGS

- The first thousand miles of England's motorway network were sketched out by official surveyors in 1938 using children's crayons on a map given away free with *Tit-Bits* magazine.

- For years, McLaren racing cars were built by Trojan, the bubble car company.

- The first Wolseley cars were manufactured by the inventor of the Maxim machine gun, in partnership with a designer of mechanized sheep-shearing equipment.

- The Frazer Nash car company was built on a fortune made by salvaging and selling unexploded World War I artillery shells.

- Vauxhall started out making engines for Thames tugs and paddle-steamers.

- AC, best known for its ferociously fast V8-engined Cobra sports cars, also built invalid carriages and the funny little train that runs the length of Southend pier.

- As part of its contribution to the war effort, Dunlop manufactured thousands of inflatable rubber Sherman tanks in the 1940s, designed to confuse German bombers.

- Long before it powered cars, petroleum was sold as a medicine, intended to 'remove pain and alleviate human suffering and disease'.

- The famous Coventry Climax engine, which went on to win three F1 World Championships, was a cleverly modified Government-issue fire pump.

- The first Ford car ever sold in England was a Model A bought by the proprietor of a home for wealthy Liverpudlian lunatics.

- Elspeth Beard, architect and the first Englishwoman to circumnavigate the world by motorcycle, lost a third of her bodyweight during her 48,000-mile epic in the 1980s. Injured in a collision with a dog, she subsequently discovered that she was fed its remains by the family that nursed her back to health.

WENT THE DAY BADLY?

According to the AA, getting lost costs motorists in this country approximately 350,000 tonnes of fuel each year. (Research by its rival the RAC similarly suggests that the average motorist wastes more than one-and-a-half hours a day sitting in the car.)

In 1950, during a demonstration for Princess Margaret at the Motor Show, Triumph chairman Sir John Black pulled the wrong lever and accidentally incinerated the sole example of the company's advanced, alloy-bodied TRX prototype.

In 1946, Anne Boleyn's prayer book and Henry VIII's dagger were stolen from Hever Castle in Kent by England's first ever ram-raiders. They were driving a Rolls-Royce.

In 1998, several Rover owners in Sutton Coldfield were left out in the cold after a stray signal from a BBC radio mast activated their central locking systems.

In August 1988, England's longest ever traffic jam stretched 22 miles from Reigate to Leatherhead along the M25.

At its launch in 1973, Reliant's Robin three-wheeler, the pride of Staffordshire, was banned from the London Motor Show because the organizing body refused to classify it as a car.

LETTING THE TRAIN TAKE THE STRAIN

- In 1969, actor Laurence Olivier led a successful campaign to see kippers back on the menu in dining cars of all London to Brighton trains.

- Old London Underground trains are still in use on the Isle of Wight where the tunnels are too small for conventional models. Running from Ryde Pier to Shanklin the nearly eighty-year-old trains clock up around 70,000 miles a year.

- In 1838 there was a Third Class, as well as First and Second, on English railways. So-called penny-passengers stood up in open wagons but could spit and smoke to their hearts' content.

- The locomotive lost in the 1879 Tay Bridge Disaster was quietly recovered, restored and reused. Staff at the North British Railway, for years the only English service to run into Scotland, called it 'the Diver'.

- In 2013 archaeologists in Derbyshire rediscovered England's oldest railway tunnel. Part of the horse-drawn Butterley Gangroad, this was built in 1793 to link the Cromford Canal with limestone quarries at Crich.

- When England's longest-serving train driver retired in 2013 at the age of sixty-seven, Bristol Temple Meads-based Bruce Parkin was estimated to have travelled 4 million miles since, at fifteen, he was first employed by British Rail to clean steam trains.

- At just over 17 miles, England's longest railway tunnel is the Northern Line running beneath London. Until 1988 it was the longest in the world.

NOT JUST WHAT THE DOCTOR ORDERED

Oh! Dr Beeching, what have you done? There once were lots of trains to catch but soon there will be none, I'll have to buy a bike, cos I can't afford a car, Oh, Dr Beeching, What a naughty man you are!

Theme tune to television sitcom *Oh! Dr Beeching* (1995–7), David Croft and Richard Spendlove

As the supposed butcher of England's railways, opprobrium continues to rain down on the head of poor Richard Beeching, whose notorious axe fell on hundreds of miles of track and an incredible 2,350 stations.

Beeching's cuts were made at a time when cheap cars led to a decline in passenger numbers and thousands of miles had already disappeared. His job was to rationalize the remaining service, while relying on equipment and technologies that were already well out of date.

Line closures, pre-Beeching			
1950	150 miles	1958	150 miles
1951	275 miles	1959	350 miles
1952	300 miles	1960	175 miles
1953	275 miles	1961	150 miles
1954 to 1957	500 miles	1962	780 miles

Line closures, post-Beeching			
1963	324 miles	1969	250 miles
1964	1,058 miles	1970	275 miles
1965	600 miles	1971	23 miles
1966	750 miles	1972	50 miles
1967	300 miles	1973	35 miles
1968	400 miles	1974	0 miles

- The Higham and Strood tunnel in Kent, part of South Eastern Railways, was originally a canal tunnel, and for a while trains ran over wooden stakes driven into the water.

- England's longest station platform, 602.6 metres, is at Gloucester. The longest station seat, at Scarborough, is 139 metres.

- Running on rails that were actually under water at high tide, the 1896 Brighton & Rottingdean Seashore Electric Tramroad was the only service ever required to carry lifejackets and a lifeboat as standard equipment.

- With a gradient too steep for most locomotives, trains had to be hauled through Liverpool's Wapping Tunnel by giant stationary steam engines. Today the steepest railway gradient is the 1 in 31.3 slope between Exeter St Davids and Exeter Central.

- The lowest point on England's railway network is at the bottom of the Severn Tunnel: 43.9 metres below sea level.

- In August 1968 when the last steam train to be operated by British Rail made its final run, it was just one day short of the 120th anniversary of George Stephenson's death.

IS IT BIRD, IS IT A PLANE, IS IT . . . A MONK?

🐾 The first Englishman to fly with wings was a Benedictine monk called Elmer of Malmesbury. According to a twelfth-century document, *Gesta regum Anglorum*, he managed to glide a furlong (around 200 metres) before breaking both his legs on landing.

🐾 British Army surgeon John Jeffries was the first to cross the English Channel by air. Travelling by balloon in January 1785 he made several observations about the weather, and something called International Weatherperson's Day is still celebrated each year on 5 February, his birthday.

🐾 The first woman in the world to pilot a powered aircraft was Englishwoman Rose Isabel Spencer. Taking the controls of 'Airship Number 1', in July 1902 she flew over Sydenham Hill in Kent.

🐾 The airship's maker Stanley Spencer subsequently flew the machine over London dropping small rubber balls on people down below. He said he did this to demonstrate to the authorities what 'the army could do with bombs'.

🐾 The first person to make a powered flight in England, and the first to hold a pilot's licence, was J. T. C. Moore-Brabazon. The death of his friend Charles Rolls persuaded him to give it up, but he hung on to the car registration FLY 1.

🐾 In 1912 C. R. Samson became the first person to take off from a moving ship when his biplane, a Short Improved S.27, left the modified deck of HMS *Hibernia*. It was to be another five years before anyone successfully landed an aircraft on the deck of a ship.

🐝 The word 'airport' was first used to describe a facility close to Southampton Docks where, sadly, the runway was built over the remains of a Roman villa. The first flight from the site was a Moonbeam II built and flown by local aviation pioneer Edwin Moon in 1910.

🐝 During the Great War aircraft design made advances very rapidly, but pilots still had such difficulty navigating that they would frequently land in fields to ask where they were, or fly low over railway lines in the hope of finding a station name-plate they could read.

🐝 After the first successful crossing by air of the Atlantic in 1919 the two pilots, one of whom was Englishman John Alcock, were knighted by George V. They also received a prize of £10,000 from the *Daily Mail*, equivalent today to £2.5 million.

🐝 Piloting a Westland's PV-3 torpedo bomber in 1933, London-born Douglas Douglas-Hamilton, the future fourteenth Duke of Hamilton, became the first person ever to fly over Mount Everest.

🐝 England's first all-female aircrew flew from Southend to Dusseldorf in 1977.

5

Sporting England

'The English are not very spiritual people so they invented cricket to give them some idea of eternity.'

George Bernard Shaw (1856–1950), playwright and author

Besides cricket the English invented a whole bunch of other sports, too – so many indeed that really the only surprise is that we rarely win at anything.

■ ■ ■

Badminton: Originally known as 'battledore and shuttlecock' the game was first played in the 1700s by English soldiers serving in India.

■ ■ ■

GAMES GONE AND BEST FORGOTTEN

Bird *v.* Bee

In 1888, the London *Daily News* carried a breathless account of a race held between bees and birds. The smart money was on the pigeons – famed for their speed, stamina and uncanny navigational abilities – but remarkably a bee was first across the line, winning by a full twenty-five seconds.

Dog *v.* Man

In 1880, a London man challenged a six-year-old retriever to a race, both of them leaping into the river below London Bridge and swimming downstream towards North Woolwich. The dog quickly gained the upper paw and by the Tower of London had a lead – a lead! – of around 50 metres. The man abandoned the chase at Wapping, and after nearly fifty minutes the dog, called Now Then, crossed the line to be declared the winner.

Sane *v.* Insane

Held in the garden of a private asylum at Fisherton in Wiltshire in 1849, the details are sketchy, but at the close of what must have been the strangest of cricket matches, the inmates were declared the winners by a margin of 61 runs.

Bride *v.* Bridesmaid

In 1899, the *Cheltenham Chronicle* reported how two factory hands staged a bicycle race in order to determine which of the two got to marry the man they both fancied. The pair competed over a two-mile course, the winner ('Nellie') claiming a white dress rather than a yellow jersey and presumably condemning the loser to wear the usual horror to which bridesmaids are traditionally subjected.

Man *v.* Bear

In 1890, 10 shillings (50p) was a handsome sum, and after a few too many beers John Picton must have thought it was worth fighting a bear for. Turns out it wasn't: the bear's owner won the wager and despite being swiftly conveyed to the London Hospital, Picton was dead on arrival.

Baseball: A diary has been found which describes the game being played by Guildford teenager William Bray on Easter Day 1755. Strange but true, America's favourite sport also gets a mention in *Northanger Abbey* (1817), Jane Austen's debut novel, in which the heroine Catherine Morland prefers 'cricket, base ball, riding on horseback and running about the country' to the more ladylike pursuit of reading.

■ ■ ■

Bowls: Swashbuckling Sir Francis Drake memorably played bowls before thrashing the Spanish and their Armada in 1588, but England's oldest green (in Southampton) dates back to at least 1299.

■ ■ ■

Bungee jumping: The first ever jump was made on April Fool's Day 1979 from Bristol's Clifton Suspension Bridge by members of the Oxford University Dangerous Sports Club.

■ ■ ■

Darts: Players of 'arrers' really did throw arrows originally, although by 1530 the sport was sufficiently well recognized for Anne Boleyn to buy a set of darts for Henry VIII.

■ ■ ■

Football: Traditionally a game for village hooligans, football was banned from 1324 to 1667, before Cambridge University devised a set of rules in the 1840s.

■ ■ ■

Ice Hockey: The game seems to have first been played in Canada, but by English soldiers.

■ ■ ■

Lawn Tennis: Clearly derived from the real or 'royal' game of Tudor times, the modern sport was devised in Edgbaston in Birmingham in the late-1800s. After Wimbledon's Centre Court, the second most famous court in the world is also in Edgbaston. It was at the University of Birmingham in 1976 that Fiona Walker was photographed scratching her bare bottom for a multi-million-selling Athena poster.

■ ■ ■

Netball: Admittedly it was derived by a Swede from the American game of basketball, but netball as we know it was first played in the 1890s at the Hampstead Physical Training College and Gymnasium, an all-women's organization in north London.

■ ■ ■

Polo: From arcane Persian roots, the modern game was devised as a training exercise for English cavalry regiments in the nineteenth century.

■ ■ ■

Rowing: As a competitive sport, rowing has its origins not in the University Boat Race but a tougher and far older event, Doggett's Coat and Badge, which has been held annually on the Thames since 1715.

■ ■ ■

Rugby: Before becoming a vicar in Essex, William Webb Ellis inadvertently invented the game after picking up the ball during a football match at the famous boys' school in 1823.

■ ■ ■

Snooker: Another game brought to England by soldiers of the empire, its name was originally army slang for a young officer.

■ ■ ■

Squash: Like its many variants, the racquet, ball and wall sport is thought to have originated with bored prisoners in London's notorious Fleet Gaol some time between 1197 when it opened and 1844 when it closed.

■ ■ ■

Table Tennis: A polite after-dinner game variously known as gossima, ping-pong and piff-paff, the first World Table Tennis Championships were held in England in 1926.

MOTORSPORT: IMPROVING THE BREED

- A former Spitfire pilot, the racing driver Robert Cowells, had an illegal sex-change operation in Harley Street in 1951. This was conceivably the first operation of its sort performed anywhere in the world.

- At the Brooklands circuit in Surrey in 1913, a Talbot became the first car to cover 100 miles in an hour but unfortunately it then toppled over, killing the driver.

- Flying round the world solo in 1930, Essex-born racing driver the Hon. Mrs Victor Bruce switched off her engine over Hong Kong to observe the two minutes' silence on Armistice Day.

- More than twenty years after it smashed the Brooklands lap record, John Cobb's mighty 24-litre Napier-Railton was employed as a mobile test-bed for military parachutes.

- Norman Culpan took a Frazer Nash to third place at Le Mans in 1949 despite never having raced a car before.

- One of the greatest racing drivers of the 1950s, Archie Scott-Brown was born without a right hand.

- Formula One star Peter Collins' memorial in St Mary's Church at Stone in Worcestershire is England's only stained glass window to incorporate a chequered flag.

- Le Mans driver Rob Walker liked to play with model cars but these so scared his dog that it once smashed through a window to get out of the way.

- Commentator Murray Walker, for many still the face of top level motor racing (see below), in a previous life as an ad man coined the slogan 'A Mars a day helps you work, rest and play'.

- The 1976 Formula One Race of Champions was banned by the BBC because the John Surtees team was sponsored by Durex.

'THERE'S NOTHING WRONG WITH HIS CAR,

EXCEPT THAT IT'S ON FIRE.'

Motorsport commentator, Murray Walker

'And Michael Schumacher is actually in a very good position. He is in last place.'

'The first three cars are all [Ford] Escorts, which isn't surprising as this is an all Escort race.'

'There's no damage to the car except to the car itself.'

'Damon Hill is following Damon Hill.'

'Excuse me while I interrupt myself.'

'He is exactly 10 seconds ahead, or more approximately, 9.86 seconds.'

'He's the only man on the track, except for his car.'

'How you can crash into a wall without it being there in the first place is beyond me.'

'I can't imagine what kind of problem Senna has. I imagine it must be some sort of grip problem.'

'Andrea de Cesaris, the man who has won more grands prix than anyone else without actually winning one of them.'

'I know it's an old cliché but you can cut the atmosphere with a cricket stump.'

'I'm ready to stop my start watch.'

'It's lap 26 of 58, which unless I'm very much mistaken is half way.'

'Jean Alesi is fourth and fifth.'

'Mansell is slowing down, taking it easy. Oh no he isn't – it's a lap record.'

Sporting England

'Only a few more laps to go and then the action will begin
unless this is the action which it is.'

'Tambay's hopes which were nil before are
absolutely zero now.'

'That's history. I say history because it happened
in the past.'

'Michael Schumacher is leading Michael Schumacher.'

'That's the first time he had started from the front
row having done so in Canada earlier this year.'

'The lead car is absolutely unique except for
the one behind it which is identical.'

'The most important part of the car is the
nut that holds the wheel.'

'Unless I am very much mistaken . . .
I am very much mistaken!'

'Villeneuve is now twelve seconds ahead of Villeneuve.'

'You might think that's not cricket, and it's not.
It's motor racing.'

YOU GO, GIRL

Historically, women have put up a pretty poor showing in Grand Prix racing, scoring just a half point between five of them since the first one had a go back in 1958. Outside Formula One, however, the stats look somewhat better, and in rallying, record-breaking, speed trials, hillclimbs and even drag racing women have more than made their mark.

Pat Moss Carlsson

The 1962 Tulip Rally was the first really big win for Minis and Mini Coopers, and saw Stirling Moss's sister Pat become the first woman to win an international rally. European Ladies' Rally Champion five times in all, she married another outstanding driver – Swedish rally ace Erik Carlsson.

Hon. Mrs Victor Bruce

As well as breaking several air and water speed records, in 1929 the aforementioned Mrs Bruce drove a 4½-litre Bentley at Montlhéry for 24 hours, capturing the world record for single-handed driving at an average of 89 mph.

Lady Mary Grosvenor

A favourite daughter of the second Duke of Westminster, Lady Mary raced regularly at Brooklands almost certainly without her father's approval. As well as hillclimbs in a Riley Sprite she championed a Bugatti Type 35, an Alta and a post-war Frazer Nash.

Violet and Evelyn Cordery

In 1929 two sisters, averaging nearly 62 mph, covered 30,000 miles round the Brooklands circuit in less than 30,000 minutes. The girls achieved this in an Invicta designed by their older sister's husband, Captain Sir Noel Macklin RNVR.

Janet Guthrie

The first woman to compete in a NASCAR superspeedway race was an American, but she did it in an English car – a 1963 Jaguar XK140 – and went on to become the first woman to take part in the legendary Indianapolis 500.

Dorothy Levitt

As well as teaching Queen Alexandra and her daughters to drive, in 1906 Levitt took the women's world speed record to 96 mph. Among her tips for her fellow lady drivers was that they consider carrying a revolver at all times.

EIGHT MEN WENT TO ROW, WENT TO ROW A RIVER . . .

- The Boat Race began in 1829 when a chap called Charles at Cambridge (Light Blue) challenged another chap called Charles from Oxford (Dark Blue). The original course was from Hambledon Lock to Henley Bridge and, captained by William Wordsworth's nephew, Oxford won.

❧ That first Oxford crew included a future bishop and the future deans of both Lincoln and Repton, while Cambridge had two future bishops, a future dean, and the future Chancellor of the Diocese of Manchester. From 1839, it became an annual fixture.

❧ The lightest ever competitor was cox Francis Archer in 1862 and the heaviest Thorsten Engelmann in 2007. Both were Cambridge men, the former tipping the scales at 32.6 kg and the latter at 110 kg.

❧ Only one race has ended in a tie – possibly because the umpire fell asleep and was unable to adjudicate – which was in 1877. Similarly, on only one occasion (1921) has the race ended with the sinking of both boats.

❧ The race was suspended for the duration of both World Wars. During the first of these every member of both 1914 crews served and half of Cambridge's winning eight – all under twenty-five – were killed, together with one Oxford man. During World War II, unofficial competitions were held at Henley-on-Thames in 1940, at Sandford-on-Thames three years later and on the River Great Ouse at Ely a year after that.

❧ Both teams have frequently relied on overseas students and in 1987 several American oarsmen mutinied after one of their number was dropped from the Oxford crew. Remarkably the latter was still victorious despite having to use a number of reserves.

❧ The tallest team in race history was Cambridge in 1999 with an average height of 6 feet 7 inches. This included the tallest ever competitor: Josh West at 6 feet 9½ inches.

- It's not unusual for brothers to compete but in 2003 Matthew Smith and David Livingston rowed for Oxford while Ben Smith and James Livingston rowed for Cambridge.

- Typically crews train for 1,200 hours, or approximately two hours per stroke needed to win the race. The current course record for a winning team is just 16 minutes and 19 seconds (Cambridge in 1998) and the slowest 26 minutes and 5 seconds (also Cambridge, in 1860).

THE MARRIAGE OF VIGORO

For those torn between the conflicting attractions of Centre Court and an afternoon at the Oval, the attempt a little over a hundred years ago to marry cricket and tennis sounds like a match made in heaven.

The game, called Vigoro, was the brainchild of J. G. Grant, a travelling salesman. He envisaged up to eleven players at a time bowling, batting and fielding, but equipped with racquets in place of the usual willow bat. With a rubber ball and six stumps rather than three, the game was advertised as suitable for both sexes. With much publicity, a 1902 event at Lord's saw a team led by tennis star E. H. Miles take on a rival eleven captained by England batsman Bobby Abel. The former team won by a good margin but the cricket authorities continued to support the game for a while before enthusiasm began to cool. After a couple of years the press admitted to losing interest, a correspondent to *The Times* noting that while 'the game certainly has some attractive features, and to watch it at a place of entertainment might be more or less interesting, one imagines that it would be the players who got the chief amusement'.

HAPPY FAMILIES

For more than two centuries and seven generations the family-run Jaques of London has dominated English games and sports from its base in south London.

As the world's oldest games and sports manufacturer it traces its descent to a French Huguenot whose son set up shop in 1795 as a 'Manufacturer of Ivory, Hardwoods, Bone and Tunbridge Ware'. Besides such delights as 'seahorse teeth' – primitive dentures made of hippo ivory – the company became known for high-quality exotic hardwoods such as ebony, lignum vitae and finest Turkey boxwood, which it used to make chessmen, croquet balls and other leisure products.

Jaques chess sets are still used for virtually every major chess tournament the world over, and the game's greatest players are all intimately familiar with the company's famous Staunton chessmen.

At the Great Exhibition of 1851 they introduced croquet from India as well as inventing numerous indoor games such as Snakes and Ladders, Tiddlywinks, Ludo and – yes – Happy Families. Later came the aforementioned Gossima (so named because the ball in play was so lightweight), which the company soon rechristened 'Ping-Pong', after inventing a table on which to play it. The same company was also the first to make resin lawn bowls, laminated glass fibre archery bows and laminated wooden tennis rackets, which transformed the game. Badminton's first featherweight steel-shafted 'four-ouncer' was also a Jaques innovation.

Undaunted by this reversal close to home, Grant hit the road again, travelling the English-speaking world to promote his idea. Over the next two decades, the game gradually morphed into a kind of cricket-baseball rather than its original tennis-cricket format, the creator modifying its equipment in the hope of sparking some interest further afield. When he died in 1927 still waiting for a breakthrough, he bequeathed the Vigoro brand to a Sydney accounts clerk called Ettie Dodge. For Grant it was his last gasp attempt to secure success and incredibly it seems to have worked: today, in at least three Australian states, a number of women's teams are still playing Vigoro.

SERIOUSLY, A GAME FOR GENTLEMEN?

To those who think football beyond the pale and rugby just snobbery with violence, the myth persists that there is something gentlemanly about cricket. Of course it's not true and never was, and for more than a hundred years the men in white have been showing they can be hooligans just as much as anyone else capable of throwing, catching, hitting or kicking a ball (or for that matter a teammate or rival).

■ ■ ■

1878: The celebrated W. G. Grace once physically manhandled another player out of the pavilion at Lord's before bundling Billy Midwinter into a cab and demanding he play for Gloucestershire at the Oval alongside Grace himself.

■ ■ ■

1911: England skipper Johnny Douglas on a visit to Melbourne City Hall told the assembled dignitaries, 'I hate speeches. As Bob Fitzsimmons once said: "I ain't no bloomin' orator, but I'll fight any man in this blinkin' country!"'

1912: Preparing for the fourth Ashes Test against England, one of the Australian selectors described team skipper Clem Hill as 'the worst captain in living memory'. Hill's response was to punch Peter McAlister in the head, before attempting to manhandle him out of a third-floor window.

■ ■ ■

1932: In the notorious 'Bodyline' Test series, the England team under the captaincy of Douglas Jardine bowled directly at Aussie batsmen in a means intended to be intimidatory and possibly injurious. Such a naked 'win at all costs' tactic was perhaps the beginning of the end of any serious consideration of the game's supposedly gentlemanly origins.

■ ■ ■

1989: Durham right-hander and occasional off-spin bowler David Boon was once reported to have consumed fifty-two cans of beer on a single plane flight. Boon has neither confirmed nor denied the story put about by Aussie fast bowler Geoff Lawson but subsequently appeared in a 'Boonanza' advertising campaign for a leading brewery.

BLUFF YOUR WAY IN WIMBLEDON

It's easy to remember: Wimbledon Fortnight always begins on the sixth Monday before the first Monday in August.

- When it began in 1877, only men were eligible, there were no doubles matches, and only twenty-two players were allowed to take part, each of whom paid a guinea (£1.05) entry fee.

- Tickets were only a shilling (5p) each even for the final, but barely 200 people turned up to see Old Harrovian Spencer Gore win the day in just 48 minutes.

- It took until 1884 before ladies were invited to play, since when the shortest of them has been Miss C. G. Hoahing, who was just 4 feet 9 inches.

- No one foreign of either sex managed to win a title at Wimbledon before 1905 and there was no prize money at all until 1968.

- The Championships were suspended during both World Wars. Centre Court was bombed five times, but standards really nose-dived when competitors were no longer required to wear full-length trousers and long dresses.

- Billie-Jean King who, together with Martina Navratilova, has won the most Wimbledon titles of anyone, received a £25 voucher for her first of twenty.

- Former British No.1 Tim Henman was the first player ever to be disqualified from Wimbledon. In 1995 he hit in anger a ball, which then struck a ball girl in the face.

- Approximately 490,000 spectators attend the Championships each year but fewer than one in three of them eat strawberries. The most important visitor is Rufus, a Harris Hawk, who flies most mornings at 9 a.m. to discourage pigeons from roosting in any of the courts.

- The only Grand Slam to be played on grass relies on a combination of 70 per cent perennial rye grass and 30 per cent Barcrown creeping red fescue, cut to a height of precisely 8 millimetres.

- No fan of tennis, the Queen has used the Royal Box only four times since her Coronation in 1953, so its seventy-four dark green Lloyd Loom wicker chairs are usually given over to celebrities and their pals.

- Players reaching the quarter-finals can afterwards claim free cups of tea for life while visiting the tournament.

6

Secret England

*'I haven't been down there myself but from what
I gather the aliens are very advanced.'*

William Francis Brinsley Le Poer Trench, eighth Earl of
Clancarty (1911–95)

Set apart from your average UFO-loon by his seat in the
upper chamber, Lord Clancarty was a former advertising
salesman with a passion for flying saucers. He believed the
mystery craft came not from outer space but from secret
bases located deep within the earth (which he believed to
be hollow).

Proof of this has so far been elusive, but, for anyone who
cares to look immediately beneath the surface of England's
green and pleasant land, there is certainly plenty of odd
stuff going on down there.

Secret wartime bunkers, tunnels no one seems to know
much about, ballrooms both underground and underwater –

all we lack is a power station carved out of a mountain, and that's only because the Welsh got there first.

Like Clancarty, who was candid enough to admit to never having visited his secret world, you may never get to see a good deal of them. Many of the best are still firmly closed to the public, but a few of the rest welcome visitors – and some are even free.

■ ■ ■

Bawburgh, Norfolk: A suspicious-looking chalet-bungalow conceals a large underground bunker, part of the Cold War-era 'Rotor' network. This codename referred to a system designed to detect attacks from Soviet nuclear bombers sneakily reverse-engineered from a Boeing B29 Superfortress which crashed in Siberia during World War II.

■ ■ ■

Bawdsey Manor, Suffolk: Now a school, this former country house was the top-secret research base at which radio direction finding (i.e. radar) was pioneered in the 1940s. The last pylon was sadly demolished to prevent it collapsing, but in deceptively peaceful surroundings several buildings remain from its time as a launch base for Bloodhound Mk II surface-to-air missiles operated by C flight, RAF No. 85 Squadron.

■ ■ ■

Beachy Head, Sussex: Caves discovered by a local vicar in the 1820s were extended and modified during World War II to provide shelter for personnel forming part of the network of so-called Centimetric Early Warning stations, which were located at strategic points around the country. The CEW bunker still exists but is blocked off and in 1963 members of the 21st SAS Territorial Regiment demolished most of the surface buildings.

■ ■ ■

Birmingham, West Midlands: Beneath Newhall Street, a network of tunnels, some more than 1,000 metres long, was constructed in the early 1950s with a specification intended to survive nuclear attack. To conceal its true purpose, the work was described to the public as being for a new metro system, but advances in weapon strength meant the tunnels were already obsolete before they were completed. Some still survive, however, and are used as underpasses and for cabling and fibre-optic communications.

■ ■ ■

Borehamwood, Hertfordshire: The Holiday Inn Elstree on Barnet bypass replaced a 1930s mock-Tudor thatched barn. During the war years this was 'Station XV' where SOE agents would prepare for missions into occupied France. These included author Pierre Boulle, two of whose novels were turned into the hit films *Bridge over the River Kwai* (1957) and *Planet of the Apes* (1968, 2001).

■ ■ ■

Bristol, Somerset: Beneath Sion Hill, the Clifton Rocks Railway, a funicular buried in the walls of the Avon Gorge, went bust in the 1930s, leaving a handy series of tunnels and caverns, which were subsequently taken over by the BBC to be used as a secret wartime transmission station.

■ ■ ■

Chelmsford, Essex: A 112-metre mast at Great Baddow is the last surviving from the pioneering radar system developed by Sir Robert Watson-Watt and his team at Bawdsey Manor (see above). As part of the Chain Home network – the given codename for a ring of early warning stations situated around the coast – it originally stood at RAF Canewdon. This was able to detect enemy aircraft while they were still in France and as the world's first integrated defence system proved to be of immeasurable value during World War II.

Corsham, Wiltshire: Codenamed 'Burlington', and excavated 40 metres below ground, this Cold War labyrinth was to be another alternative seat of power if London was threatened or disabled by nuclear strike. For more than thirty years it remained top secret, until the 1980s when it was outed by a *Guardian* journalist. Carved out of a disused quarry, the vast complex of tunnels, shafts and chambers extends for more than half a mile below ground and could accommodate 4,000 people for up to three months. Unfortunately, the advent of intercontinental ballistic missiles rendered it redundant by the time it was completed, and by 2004 it was home to a skeleton staff of just four.

■ ■ ■

Dover, Kent: Beneath the famous castle, a network of tunnels dates back to Napoleonic times and possibly even earlier. Later extensions to these provided a base for 'Dumpy', the joint-service HQ for the evacuation of Dunkirk ('Operation Dynamo') and more recently it housed an important NATO communications centre. The labyrinth extends to around 3 miles and includes old anti-aircraft plotting rooms, wireless links to airfields and naval bases, and – best of all – a BBC transmitter intended to broadcast pacifying music once Soviet missiles were known to be on their way.

■ ■ ■

Edge Hill, Liverpool: Excavated by a local property owner in the early 1800s an extraordinary subterranean tangle incorporates a mass of tunnels, some of which are as much as 6 metres high. Much of the layout was mapped by members of the West Lancashire Territorial Forces although its purpose remains mysterious.

■ ■ ■

Eton College, Berkshire: Perhaps one shouldn't be surprised that the school offers its pupils every conceivable facility – including a nuclear bunker, although like all of its 1950s peers this was declared obsolete as soon as it was completed. With room for just fifty in a school of well over a thousand, one wonders what were the entry criteria.

■ ■ ■

Folkestone, Kent: Below Shakespeare Cliff lie the remains of the first attempt at digging a Channel tunnel. In 1881, railway pioneer Sir William Watkin formed the Submarine Continental Railway Tunnel Company in order to explore the feasibility of a tunnel linking England and France. Employing the splendidly named Beaumont-English Boring Machine, he subsequently excavated more than 2,000 metres before money ran out and fears were raised about a possible French invasion. Incredibly, a quarter of the tunnel still remains, although it is locked, partly flooded and extremely hazardous to enter.

■ ■ ■

Fylingdales, Yorkshire: As part of the Ballistic Missile Early Warning System, three highly visible radomes or 'golfballs' work with two sister stations in Greenland and Alaska to track spy satellites as well as missile attacks. The theory is that by knowing when and where enemy satellites are, NATO forces can carry out specific operations when they are other than overhead.

■ ■ ■

Gants Hill, Essex: In one of the more extraordinary schemes of the 1940s, 2½ miles of twin tunnel between Gants Hill and Newbury Park were turned over to the Plessey Company for conversion into a top-secret armaments factory. Both tunnels are now used to run Central Line trains into London.

Gilsland, Cumbria: The remains of RAF Spadeadam include few buildings but surviving elements scattered around the forest include the raw concrete of several rocket engine test-stands, concrete control bunkers and at Greymare Hill two vast, bleak rocket stands. These date from the halcyon days of British rocketry before the adoption of the US Thor missile in 1958 led to the cancellation of our own Blue Streak programme. For years the 9,000-acre site – the RAF's largest – was so secret that when tree-felling uncovered the location of a missile silo in 2004 no one from English Heritage nor the RAF was able to find any blueprints for it.

■ ■ ■

Hawthorne, Wiltshire: In disused Bath stone quarries underlying RAF Rudloe Manor, a secret factory was established by the armaments maker BSA during World War II. In caverns extending to more than 200,000 square metres the company manufactured and assembled thousands of badly needed M1919 Browning machine guns. During the Cold War, the facility housed part of the organization charged with providing the public with the four-minute warning of any enemy attack.

■ ■ ■

HMY *Britannia* (at sea): Rumours of escape tunnels beneath Buckingham Palace remain unproven, but there were plans for the royal yacht to serve as a mobile bunker in the event of a nuclear war. With Her Majesty on board together with Prince Philip and the Home Secretary the vessel would have hidden in the sea lochs on Scotland's west coast. The party would not have included the PM because, in the event of his or her death, the sovereign is required to appoint a replacement.

■ ■ ■

Kidderminster, Worcestershire: The Drakelow Tunnels beneath Kingsford Country Park provided thousands of square metres of space for armaments manufacture during World War II. Initially aircraft components were made here by the Rover Car Company, and during the Cold War the facility was repurposed by the Home Office for use as a Regional Centre of Government. Now decommissioned, it was more recently raided by the police following a tip-off that part of it was being used to grow cannabis.

■ ■ ■

Kingstanding, Sussex: A prominent pylon above a bunker near Crowborough was used for years by the BBC World Service. However, it was originally operated by the Political Warfare Executive in the 1940s to broadcast black propaganda to occupied Europe.

■ ■ ■

Lakenheath, Suffolk: A tenth of Britain's 300 post-war airbases were leased to the US Strategic Air Command, and for a while as one of the largest, Lakenheath was home to two Lockheed U2 spy planes. In 1956 it came close to nuclear catastrophe when a Boeing B-47 Stratojet crashed into a storage 'igloo' containing several atomic weapons. Fortunately these did not have their fissile cores installed, although between them they contained 10 tonnes of high explosives. Incredibly no denotation occurred but four crewmen were killed and the damaged weapons were shortly afterwards removed from the base by the Atomic Energy Commission.

■ ■ ■

Rochester, Kent: From the Esplanade at Rochester it is possible to see the traces of another underground aircraft factory, this one commissioned in the 1940s by Short Brothers for the construction of seaplanes well away from enemy eyes and aircrews. Extensive tunnels and ventilation shafts were cut into chalk cliffs and lined with brick. With air-raid shelters and storage and another 400-metre tunnel connecting the new facility to the existing aircraft factory, it remained in use as storage until the 1990s. Since then most of the area has been blocked off and backfilled.

■ ■ ■

Rochester, Kent: The large Parcelforce depot overlies a site with military connections dating back to 1860, when Fort Bridgewater was built here to protect Chatham Dockyard. Successively updated, with two companion forts it provided anti-aircraft cover during World War II before it was modified to withstand an A-bomb attack in the 1950s.

■ ■ ■

Witley Park, Surrey: Situated between Godalming and Haslemere, the convicted financial fraudster Whitaker Wright spent millions moving hills, planting forests, building a vast country house and excavating a dramatic quartet of decorative lakes. Beneath one of these lies England's only underwater ballroom, reached via a secret door in a false tree, then a tunnel, a spiralling ramp, and finally another tunnel navigable only by boat. Its creator killed himself in the dock at the Old Bailey, and his house burnt down.

■ ■ ■

Worksop, Nottinghamshire: In an area of the country still known as the Dukeries, the fifth Duke of Portland (1800–79) employed 15,000 workers and built an underground ballroom, an underground riding school with room for 100 horses (he never rode), three underground libraries each of which was painted pink, and a series of tunnels so that His Grace could travel around and out of his estate without being seen.

THE NAME'S BOND, JOHN BOND

It seems that the inspiration for England's most celebrated spy dates from long before his first fictional appearance in the 1930s.

Ian Fleming got the name for his bestselling creation from a copy of *Birds of the West Indies* (1936) by ornithologist James Bond. In 2008, an old diary emerged describing the exploits of John Bond, an Elizabethan secret agent whose family even share the fictional Bond's motto: *Non Sufficit Orbis* ('The World Is Not Enough').

The diary was written by Bond's son Denis, a member of a family still prominent in the area of Dorset where Ian Fleming went to prep school before attending Eton College.

Denis reveals how his father worked undercover for queen and country, accompanying Sir Francis Drake on several missions, including an assault in 1586 on the Spanish Azores. He also describes Bond Senior's escape during the 1573 Bartholomew's Day Massacre in France. More Sean Connery than Roger Moore, his father reputedly threatened to kill a woman and her child before ransoming them both in order to secure his own safe passage.

Besides the Dorset connection, Fleming frequently took names and events from real life. Among his villains, the man with the golden gun was named after a fellow Etonian called Scaramanga, while the brutalist architect Erno Goldfinger – no friend of Fleming's – resurfaced as namesake Auric in the adventure of the same name.

7

Island England

Famously an 'island nation', England's tally may fall far short of Scotland's – 790, of which around a sixth are inhabited – but the English coastline throws up many islands more peculiar than the mainland's inhabitants would guess.

Lundy, Bristol Channel

With a resident population of twenty-eight, Lundy has been inhabited since the Bronze Age – possibly not continuously – and was invaded by Henry III when one William de Marisco set himself up as king. Passing through several different owners, including the Knights Templar and one who illegally introduced his own currency, it is now in the care of the National Trust and offers a variety of unusual holiday accommodation for non-smokers.

Asparagus Island, Cornwall

Named after the vegetable which grows wild here, Asparagus can be reached at low tide by walking across a tombolo, a stretch of sandy beach which the sea laps on both sides.

Godrevy Island, Cornwall

Said to have inspired the high-modernist novel *To The Lighthouse* by Virginia Woolf, Godrevy was also the scene of the mysterious discovery within 15,000-year-old Ice Age deposits of a dog skeleton shown to be no more than 400 years old.

Looe Island, Cornwall

Said locally to have been visited by a young Jesus and his father, in the twentieth century the island was bought by two unmarried sisters. They continued to live on the island until they were in their late eighties, bequeathing it to a nature conservancy charity on their deaths.

Piel Island, Cumbria

The landlord of the eighteenth-century Ship Inn is traditionally known as the 'King of Piel', his three subjects making this the twentieth most heavily populated island in England. The last time there was a 'coronation' the story got coverage as far away as Japan but the real kings are the dukes of Buccleuch. At least they were until 1920 when the seventh of that line gave his island to the people of Barrow-in-Furness as a memorial to those of them who fell in the Great War.

Roa Island, Cumbria

With a population of around a hundred, Roa's most famous inhabitant was industrialist Henry Schneider (1817–87). At one point the world's largest steel producer, he was an MP until he was found to have bribed voters. His luxurious steam yacht *Esperance* was the model for the boat in Arthur Ransome's *Swallows and Amazons* (1930).

Walney Island, Cumbria

The largest of the Isles of Furness and by far the most populous with more than 10,000 residents, the large settlement of Vickerstown was built and named by the famous armaments manufacturer. Choosing a mock-Tudor style it offered accommodation of a quality much higher than ordinary shipworkers would expect, but use of the bridge connecting the island to the mainland required the payment of a toll.

Burgh Island, Devon

This tidal island's Art Deco hotel replaced an old pilchard-fishing community and provided an atmospheric setting for Agatha Christie's *Ten Little Niggers* and *Evil Under the Sun*. It is almost certainly the only chic hotel in the country where it's de rigueur to arrive by tractor, a specially adapted 1960s Fordson being employed to carry guests across the saturated sand.

Drake's Island, Devon

Comprising a mix of lava and limestone, the island is named after the swashbuckling Plymouth privateer who was made governor after his 1580 global circumnavigation. In 1665, one of Charles I's murderers was sentenced to die here, and in 1774 a carpenter called John Day became the world's first submarine fatality when his homemade wooden chamber failed.

Great Mew Stone, Devon

The subject of several paintings by J. M. W. Turner (*The Mewstone* forms part of the Tate's Turner Bequest), this little wedge-shaped outcrop is uninhabited. Proximity to HMS *Cambridge* Gunnery School placed it out of bounds to the public during World War II and as an important bird sanctuary it is still closed to visitors.

Brownsea Island, Dorset

The birthplace of a global movement, 'Branksea' was the location of the 1907 trial camp at which Lieutenant-General R. S. S. Baden-Powell and his 'Mafeking Cadets' set out to test ideas for his book *Scouting for Boys*. In the 1920s, those living on Brownsea were forcibly repatriated to the mainland by its reclusive owner, Mary Bonham-Christie, and visitors were more or less banned until her death in the 1960s. One of those kept away was Enid Blyton, but viewing it from afar she used Brownsea as the model for 'Kirrin Island' in her *Famous Five* children's books. As a grey-squirrel-free island it is one of the last refuges in the south of the native red.

Gigger's Island, Dorset

Almost lost in Poole Harbour, this is the world's third largest natural harbour, after New Zealand's Kaipara Harbour and San Francisco Bay, California.

Canvey Island, Essex

Cut off from the mainland by a series of small creeks but connected to it by two road bridges, Canvey was briefly the capital of 1970s pub-rock, both as home to Dr Feelgood and a destination for others active in the genre. Architecturally it is ugly, but the Lobster Smack inn is mentioned in Charles Dickens' *Great Expectations* (1860), and for lovers of thirties modernism, the Grade II-listed Labworth Café is thrilling.

Cindery Island, Essex

Situated off the mouth of Brightlingsea Creek, this uninhabited patch lent its name to the graphic novel *Captain Swing and the Electrical Pirates Of Cindery Island* (2011) by local author and resident (and 'Iron Man' co-creator) Warren Ellis.

Foulness Island, Essex

This lonely corner of creek-cut Essex has a population of around 200, but no church or pub since 2010. Until 1922 it could be reached only along the Broomway, a 2,000-year-old track across treacherous tidal sands. Extending to a little over 9 square miles the island is still administered on behalf of the Ministry of Defence so that non-residents must apply for a pass to visit. Most who do visit come to see the birds as it is a nationally important site for many migratory species.

Havengore Island, Essex

An isolated spot on the way to Foulness notable for the discovery in 2000 of what are believed to be the remains of HMS *Beagle*. Darwin's survey ship is thought in retirement to have been used to block a channel of the River Roach, serving as a watch house for coastguard officers charged with preventing smuggling along this stretch of coast.

Island England

Horsey Island, Essex

Arthur Ransome's popular *Swallows and Amazons* series is most closely associated with the Lake District, but the author spent time sailing off the Essex and Suffolk saltmarshes. His Bermuda-rigged cutter *Nancy Blackett* is still moored at Woodbridge in Suffolk and in 1939 Horsey Island made an appearance in *Secret Water*. It is still privately owned.

Mersea Island, Essex

Cut off each high tide, pedestrians and road vehicles all use an astonishing piece of seventh-century engineering called the Strood, a Saxon causeway requiring the sinking of more than 3,000 oak piles. The Great War claimed the lives of one in six Mersea men and today the most easterly of England's inhabited islands is unequally divided between sailors (in the west) and caravanners to the east. Its oysters are Europe's finest.

Northey Island, Essex

Situated in the Blackwater estuary, in AD 991 the island was popularly supposed to be where Aethelred the Unready was forced to pay the first instalment of *Danegeld*, a fine payable to the invading Norsemen after losing the Battle of Maldon. Today it is a bird reserve with a human population of one.

Osea Island, Essex

Northey's neighbour – both are reached along tidal causeways – was offered for sale a few years ago for £6 million. A previous owner, a scion of the Charrington brewing family, attempted to run the island as a teetotal retreat in the early 1900s. This failed when a carter, employed to smuggle spirits to the residents, lost his way on the causeway and drowned.

THE SHINGLES CHARTS – OR THOSE WHICH NEVER QUITE MADE IT TO ISLAND STATUS

Blakeney Point, Norfolk
A four-mile shingle bank, home to 500 harbour and grey seals and 187 different species of beetle.

Calshot Spit, Hampshire
Fortified by Henry VIII (whose castle still stands) the spit was later used by Royal Navy and Royal Air Force seaplanes and flying boats.

Chesil Beach, Dorset
Views of the 18-mile shingle structure were recently voted the third best in England by readers of *Country Life*.

Dungeness, Kent
For years one of the weirdest and remotest places in south-east England the area is now favoured by trendy Londoners upgrading the old cottages – some of them railway carriages – which litter what Met. Office data suggests is Britain's only desert.

Hurst Spit, Hampshire
In 1648 the Henrician fort here was used to hold Charles I prisoner before he was escorted to London and murdered.

Mudeford Spit, Dorset
Site of the infamous Black House which features in many legends of smugglers sticking it to the authorities. In fact it was built in the 1840s for a senior employee of the Hengistbury Head Mining Company, meaning the tales are all tosh.

Orford Ness, Suffolk

Europe's largest vegetated shingle spit was for years an outpost of the Atomic Weapons Research Establishment. Visitors can still see the extraordinary 'pagodas' used to test nuclear-bomb components and a genuine (disarmed) weapon from the 1960s.

Spurn Head, Yorkshire

The location of Henry of Bolingbroke landing in 1399, before his attempt to unseat his cousin Richard II. In this he was successful and reigned as Henry IV.

Rushley Island, Essex

Still privately owned, in the 1700s the island was farmed by John Harriot (1745–1817), a local seafarer from Rochford. He was the founder of the Marine Police Force on the River Thames, the first constabulary anywhere in the world, and served in the Seven Years War before becoming shipwrecked on the aforementioned Great Mew Stone.

Whale Island, Essex

Home to HMS *Excellent*, the Royal Navy's oldest 'stone frigate' or shore establishment. This was created in the early nineteenth century as a training base to improve the Navy's woefully poor record for accurate and effective gunnery.

Baker's Island, Hampshire

The site of a 'Starfish Decoy', a 1940s initiative to confuse enemy bombers using elaborate light displays in remote areas to simulate the appearance of towns and cities. An estimated 968 tons of German ordnance was wasted as a result.

Isle of Wight, Hampshire

Strictly speaking the Isle of Man, 'wight' being Middle English for a sentient being. England's largest island at almost 150 square miles but only its second most populous, after Portsea.

Bryher, Isles of Scilly

Walkable from Tresco at low tide, the island will be familiar to viewers of *The Voyage of the Dawn Treader* (1989).

Gugh, Isles of Scilly

The location of Obadiah's Barrow, one of around eighty burial chambers in the Scilly Isles. This one contains several cremation urns and a crouching Bronze Age skeleton. The Old Man of Gugh is a 2.7-metre menhir, or standing stone, at the foot of Kittern Hill.

Ragged Island, Isles of Scilly

Known for mysterious growths of Chilean hard-fern (*Blechnum cordatum*), a species largely confined to the southern hemisphere.

St Agnes, Isles of Scilly

Joined to Gugh by a tombolo, St Agnes is assumed to be the last resting place of many of the victims of the Scilly naval disaster of 1707 in which four warships and more than 1,400 sailors went down in a storm.

St Helen's, Isles of Scilly

An intriguing ruin is the 1764 Pest House related to a 1754 Act of Parliament requiring any plague-ridden ships north of Cape Finisterre in Spain to anchor off the island.

St Martin's, Isles of Scilly

Located on the island is a so-called daymark, an unusual circular tower intended to be visible to shipping in daylight in much the same way that a lighthouse functions at night.

Samson, Isles of Scilly

Named after St Samson of Dol, a fifth-century religious figure who refrained from alcohol after his predecessor as Abbot of Caldy got drunk and fell down a well.

Isle of Sheppey, Kent

With a population of around 38,000, Kent's largest island boasts three prisons.

Lindisfarne, Northumberland

A base for Christian evangelism since being settled by St Aiden in AD 634. The locals have still not forgiven the British Museum for running off with the *Lindisfarne Gospels*, although they now have an impeccable copy of the richly illustrated text.

Birnbeck Island, Somerset

Connected by pier to the mainland, an arrangement unique in England. In the 1940s it was home to the deliberately mysterious-sounding Admiralty Directorate of Miscellaneous Weapons Development.

Stert Island, Somerset

Proudly the last place in England where wooden sledges or mudhorses are pulled across the mudflats to collect fish from nets.

Hayling Island, West Sussex

Windsurfing was invented here in 1958, a fact now established in law. A year later Her Serene Highness Princess Catherine Yurievskaya, the youngest daughter of Tsar Alexander II, died on the island, her home for many years.

Thorney Island, West Sussex

Separated from the mainland by a channel called the Great Deep, RAF Thorney Island was successively a fighter base, a part of Coastal Command charged with protecting shipping in the English Channel, a Fleet Air Arm base testing novel aircraft, and is now assigned to the Royal Regiment of Artillery.

8

Inventing England

'Innovation is serendipity, so you don't know what people will make.'

Tim Berners-Lee, inventor of the World Wide Web

The news in mid-2014 that a man from Lincolnshire had built the world's largest fart machine (and aimed it squarely at France) was proof that we're still one of the great inventing nations. It's true that not everyone can be like Henry Shrapnel, Alex Moulton or James Dyson and get his name on a product, but in the country that gave the world the anti-garrotting cravat, there are still thousands of inspired and creative Englishmen and women, beavering away in sheds, waiting for their moment in the sun.

IN BUSINESS

🐾 Scots like to boast that it was one of their countrymen who paved the way for the creation of the Bank of England but choose to forget that the Bank of Scotland was founded by John Holland, a sailor's son from London.

🐾 The world's first synthetic organic dye was invented by accident by eighteen-year-old William Henry Perkin. Whilst attempting to synthesize a cure for malaria, he created something called mauveine. Renamed mauve, this proved a popular food colourant and fabric dye, especially when Queen Victoria wore it to her daughter's wedding.

🐾 Everyone knows Thomas Edison invented the lightbulb, except perhaps Thomas Edison. Recognizing that he had been beaten to it by Englishman Sir Joseph Swan the great man called in the lawyers, then changed his mind and instead proposed that the two of them merge their companies.

🐾 An American, Hiram Maxim, is credited with the invention of the first machine gun in 1884. In fact, an Englishman had beaten him to it more than 150 years earlier. Lawyer James Puckle patented the first, bizarrely choosing bullets which were square rather than round in cross-section, and specifying that these were to be used only for killing Ottoman Turks. This made the bullets both slow and inaccurate, and the project was not a success.

🐾 Once an invaluable aid to office secretaries everywhere, the world's first shorthand – what a contemporary called 'a speedie kinde of wryting by Character' – was invented in the 1580s by the physician and clergyman Timothie Bright.

- It took another 200 years for someone to invent the eraser. Optician Edward Nairne reached for breadcrumbs – used throughout the eighteenth century to rub out pencil marks – but picked up a piece of rubber by mistake and found it worked rather better.

- Documents prove that by 1714 Henry Mill had 'by his great study and paines & expence invented and brought to perfection an artificial machine or method for impressing or transcribing of letters, one after another' – but sadly no more is known of the world's first typewriter and no example of it has survived.

- The magnetron sounds more like the worst kind of sci-fi hokum, but its invention by Sir John Randall and Dr Harry Boot of Birmingham University led directly to the microwave oven.

- Sylvanus Urban, the pen-name of London publisher Edward Cave, was the first to produce a general-interest magazine. This was *The Gentleman's Magazine*, a monthly digest which from 1731 collected together articles on many diverse subjects hence the choice of its title from the Arabic نزاخم or *makhazin* meaning a storehouse.

A WORLD ON WHEELS (AND TRACKS) (AND AIR)

Bicycles are faster, lighter, use sexier materials and are consequently hugely more expensive than ever before, but the arrangement of a diamond frame and two similar-sized wheels really hasn't changed much since 1885. John Kemp Starley introduced the concept with his Rover safety cycle, a design which proved so influential that in Poland bikes are still referred to as 'rowers'.

It's rival the Ivel of 1886 was designed by a Bedfordshire man, Dan Albone, who also built the world's first practical tractor. A keen racing cyclist in his spare time, he became the first man ever to be penalized in an event for using newfangled inflatable tyres.

The first mountain bike was built in the mid-1960s by Geoff Apps, who had become tired of the noise and disturbance caused by motorcycles during off-road trials in the Chiltern Hills.

■ ■ ■

John Fowler (1826–64) failed in his attempt to produce smokeless steam engines for use on the London Underground, but after witnessing the effects of the Irish potato famine designed the world's first steam drainage plough. Sadly, not long after pioneering such an important move into mechanized agriculture, he fell off his horse and died of his injuries.

■ ■ ■

The baby's perambulator or pram was designed in 1733 by the Palladian architect William Kent for his client, the fourth Duke of Devonshire. To save any exertions on the part of His Grace, the wheeled basket was designed to be pulled by a goat. Patented in the mid-1960s, the first collapsible buggy was also English, Saffron Walden-born Owen Maclaren having previously designed the undercarriage for the Supermarine Spitfire.

■ ■ ■

After experimenting with a little spring-powered toy on a reservoir outside London, farmer Francis Petit Smith was the first to fit a propeller to a boat. It broke the first time he tried it but even in its damaged condition made the canal barge go twice as fast as its inventor had predicted.

Light enough to be pulled by a single horse, and intended to be sufficiently agile so it could weave a path through heavy traffic, the Hansom cab revolutionized urban travel and paved the way for today's taxi trade. It was the brainchild of Joseph Hansom, another architect, but bizarrely it was first used not in London but in Hinckley, Leicestershire.

■ ■ ■

Born in Bath in 1744, Richard Lovell Edgeworth designed 'a cart that carries its own road'. He spent so long fiddling around with the design – at least forty years – that by the time he had perfected what we call caterpillar tracks, several others had beaten him to the patent office. Among the things distracting him were four wives and their twenty-two children.

■ ■ ■

The diesel engine is assumed to have been invented by Rudolf Diesel in 1897, but it should really be called the Akroyd-Stuart engine. Diesel's engine used coal dust as fuel, but the oil-burning device we know and rely on today was patented by a Yorkshireman, Herbert Akroyd-Stuart, at least five years earlier.

■ ■ ■

Francis Herbert Wenham (1824–1908) built the world's first wind tunnel back in 1871 but vehicle aerodynamics were so poorly understood that more than sixty years later, the average car was still more efficient when driving backwards rather than forwards.

■ ■ ■

The hovercraft was invented in 1955 by Christopher Cockerell, who successfully proved the concept using two tin cans and a vacuum cleaner. He was rebuffed by both the marine industry, which dismissed it as an aircraft, and the aviation industry, which looked upon it as a boat.

Resurgam, the world's first practical submarine, was invented by Manchester vicar George Garrett. Unfortunately, it went down in Liverpool Bay in 1880 and despite its name – Latin for 'I shall rise again' – didn't return to the surface. In fact, the submarine remained lost for the next 115 years, until it was discovered by an amateur diver called Keith.

■ ■ ■

In 1784 an Essex man, Lionel Ludkin, was awarded the patent for the first ever lifeboat which used airtight cork-filled containers to ensure its buoyancy. It is conceivable that a Geordie called William Woodhave beat him to it, but he was too poor to test his ideas and too foul-mouthed to win the support of anyone with the resources to help him.

MASTERS OF THE MUSICK

- The great Italian violin makers (Stradivari, Guarneri, the Amati brothers) are believed to have acquired the tricks of the trade from a Jewish luthier expelled from medieval Spain. It was Englishman James Tubbs who created the perfect bow, and today examples of his work can command tens of thousands of pounds. As with a 'Strad', the secret's in the varnish, they say: something Tubbs reportedly cooked up using stale urine.

- The traditional concertina, or squeeze-box, was invented in 1829 by Sir Charles Wheatstone. Six-sided, with sixty-four keys, it provided a pleasant diversion from his other activities which included devising a secret military encryption technique (one which was still in use by British Intelligence more than a century later) and a sophisticated means of electric telegraphy.

The pBone, the world's first plastic trombone, was invented by Warwickshire musician and engineering graduate Hugh Rashleigh. It's robust and cheap to make, yet matches the sound of all but the world's best brass instruments. More importantly, you can buy the world's bestselling trombone in yellow, green, red, blue, purple, black, white, orange or pink.

AS IF WITH ONE VOICE

For all its American associations, the first ever Glee Club was established in 1787 at Harrow School, Middlesex, for the improvement of vocal harmony among the English upper classes. Popular until the mid-1850s, with most schools participating in the tradition, choral societies eventually took over. 'Glee' refers to short English songs sung by trios or quartets in parts, rather than the mood in which they are sung.

The Wurlitzer Theatre Organ, made famous by the New York manufacturer of the same name, was the creation of Robert Hope-Jones who devised what he called his 'Unit-Orchestra' after serving an apprenticeship at Laird's Shipbuilders in Birkenhead. He built nearly 250 of the instruments himself before merging with Wurlitzer, a move he so much regretted that he killed himself shortly afterwards.

- The Logical Bassoon, an electronically controlled version of the traditional woodwind instrument, was invented in the late 1960s by the composer and physician Giles Brindley. An expert in erectile dysfunction, Dr Brindley wanted an instrument that sounded the same yet was easier to play, but commercial success somehow eluded the finished product.

- A trumpeting friend to Purcell and Handel, John Shore (1662–1752) invented the tuning fork. Besides being used to tune musical instruments, it provides the time-keeping element in many electronic watches, is used by doctors to test hearing, practitioners of alternative medicine for all sorts of nonsense, and by traffic police to calibrate speed guns.

A MAN NEEDS A HOBBY

- In 1913, Liverpool-born journalist Arthur Wynne invented the 'word-cross', or as we now call it the crossword.

- The hobby of philately was invented by zoologist John Edward Grey, who bought some Penny Blacks with the specific intention of keeping them instead of using them. He did this on 1 May 1840, the first day the stamps were ever offered for sale.

- The world's first trainspotter was Jonathan Backhouse, who watched the inaugural journey of the world's first public railway (the Stockton to Darlington Railway, in September 1825) before noting down details to share with his sister.

CRYPTOZOOLOGICAL MONSTERS

The concept of creative taxidermy came from nineteenth-century Yorkshire squire Charles Waterton. His innovations included the Noctifer, made from bits of an eagle owl combined with others from a bittern, the Nondescript – a dried howler monkey which looked disturbingly like a miniature mummified eskimo – and something he described as 'John Bull and the National Debt'. This had a vaguely human face with the body of a porcupine and the shell of a tortoise.

(Waterton also invented artificial nesting boxes, which he distributed around his estate to encourage birds to roost. It's not hard to imagine why they might have stayed away.)

- The term birdwatching was coined in 1901 by Edmund Selous, an ornithologist now celebrated but not well known during his lifetime, as he preferred not to mix with anyone who shared his interests.

- Plasticine was invented in 1897 by an art teacher looking for a type of non-drying clay with which his students could practise. William Harbutt went into commercial production two years later. The stuff is now made in Thailand.

- The world's first bodybuilding contest was held at the Royal Albert Hall in 1901. In simpler, pre-steroid times, participants were called upon to mimic Classical-era statues for the judges who included Sir Arthur Conan Doyle and a German, Eugen Sandow, who presented the eventual winner with a sculpture of himself.

- The idea of mountaineering as a hobby rather than as a means to an end began in 1886 with the successful conquest of Napes Needle in the Lake District by Old Etonian W. P. Haskett Smith.

- Airfix originally produced combs and inflatable toys, and only moved into plastic construction kits after being asked to model a Ferguson TE20 tractor in 1949. Its first aircraft took another six years to launch, the boss being convinced that no one would want to build a model Spitfire.

- The first choir competition was held in 1719, between choristers from Hereford, Gloucester and Worcester cathedrals. It still takes place each August and is thought to be the world's oldest music festival.

- Gongoozling, which involves hanging around locks and canals while doing not very much really, made its first appearance in a 1944 book *Narrow Boat* by L. T. C. Rolt. It is thought to have been derived from canalworkers' slang for an onlooker, the sort of person who loiters by a pair of lockgates while someone does all the work.

IT'S A MATERIAL WORLD

- Coade Stone, an exceptionally durable artificial stone used in eighteenth- and nineteenth-century buildings, was created by Mrs Eleanor Coade. She mixed crushed flint, quartz and glass with clay and firesand (or 'grog') to produce stoneware that could be easily moulded and has proved to be incredibly resistant to wear and tear.

🌂 Parkesine, the first commercially produced plastic, was invented in 1856 by Birmingham metallurgist Alexander Parkes. It would have been a rival for Bakelite but for its unfortunate tendency to explode without warning.

🌂 Portland cement was invented in Leeds in 1824 and gained the name only because it was thought similar in appearance to the famous Dorset stone. Mixed from ground limestone and clay, its ability to withstand immersion in water (and possibly even to become stronger when wet) made it the material of choice for Victorian sewer builders.

🌂 Whilst attempting to devise a new corrosion-resistant alloy for a weapons manufacturer, Harry Brearley stumbled upon stainless steel in 1913. Initially marketed as 'Staybrite', one of the first applications for the new miracle metal was the famous awning over the entrance to London's Savoy Hotel.

🌂 Another accidental discovery was polythene, which emerged from a contaminated experiment conducted at ICI in Cheshire in 1933. Because it was used to insulate cables which formed part of top-secret radar equipment, any potential commercial applications of the new material were outlawed until after the war.

🌂 The first strong, lightweight carbon fibre was first created by the Royal Aircraft Establishment at Farnborough in Hampshire in 1963. Used in everything from tennis clubs through bullet-proof vests to Formula One cars, it is stronger than steel when stretched or bent, but struck with a hammer can easily shatter.

The English can't claim to have invented camouflage but perhaps suspicious of its Frenchified name (thought to be from *camoufler*, Parisian slang, meaning to disguise something) the army introduced something called Disruptive Pattern Material in the 1960s. As such they were the first force anywhere in the world to adopt a universal design of disguising uniform.

ORGANIZATIONS

The Young Men's Christian Association or YMCA was established in 1844 by a London shop assistant. George Williams observed that for 'men engaged in the drapery, embroidery, and other trades', their time off seemed to revolve around pubs and prostitutes. His solution was to offer them prayer meetings and Bible-readings, which proved enormously popular. Within five or six years the 'Y' had branches in Australia, Belgium, Canada, France, Germany, Holland, Switzerland and the USA.

Established in 1907, Lt Gen. Robert Baden-Powell's Scout movement drew ideas from the American Woodcraft Indians and the Scottish founder of the Boys' Brigades. Together with the Girl Guides it rapidly outgrew both, and today there are thought to be around 40 million members worldwide of both sexes.

Originally intending to recruit only alcoholics, drug addicts and prostitutes, William Booth's Salvation Army began as a Methodist mission in east London in 1885. It was one of the first church organizations to give women equal preaching rights with men, but for years members were forbidden to marry anyone who wasn't also a Salvation Army member.

BACK TO BLACK

Created in a Surrey laboratory using carbon nanotubes that were discovered in the 1990s, a new material called Vantablack is the blackest substance known to man. It cannot be processed by human vision, so that shapes and contours are lost and it looks as though there is nothing there, the closest thing to a black hole we can so far experience. Vantablack reflects just 0.035 per cent of any light shone on it – for a comparison, matt-black charcoal reflects more than one hundred times as much. So far, no one except artists Anish Kapoor really seems to know what they would want to do with it, although a Belgian artist, Frederik de Wilde, claims he might have got there first with his works of Nano Black, which he formed in collaboration with NASA.

9

Aristocratic England

'Whether democracy or aristocracy is the better form of government constitutes a very difficult question.'

Alexis de Tocqueville (1805–59),
French political thinker and historian

Everyone loves a lord, or so they say, but in a country where it's acceptable to dismiss someone as a toff but never to write them off as a pleb, the upper classes could be forgiven for thinking they are under attack like never before. In the face of this new peasants' revolt, most have sensibly retreated. Rarely to their country estates – thousands of which have disappeared or changed hands in recent decades – and obviously not to the House of Lords, which is barred to all but a few of them. Most have just withdrawn from public life, which is a shame because over many centuries they've not done a bad job while providing the country with some much needed colour as well as the odd controversy.

THEIR LORDSHIPS' HOUSE

- No longer a happy bastion of inherited privilege, the House of Lords nevertheless retains its peculiarities. It has more members than the House of Commons, and rather more women. It is also able to put a brake on legislation passing through the Commons, although MPs can stop them doing this by invoking the Parliament Act of 1911.

- The red carpet in the corridors (like the red leather benches in the chamber itself) matches the colour of the adjacent Lambeth Bridge. Westminster Bridge similarly echoes the green carpets and green benches of the House of Commons, although the reasons for this are now lost in the mists of time.

- Members convicted of crimes – such as recent cases of perjury and fiddling expenses – are not barred from sitting in the chamber following their release. Nor, like peers who are declared bankrupt, can they be stripped of their titles or fired. Because of this, convicted criminals can still 'clock-in' and collect £300 each time they do so – equivalent to a job paying £150,000 a year.

- Until 1999, peers were forbidden even to sit in the House of Commons and yet the job of prime minister has been given to a duke on eight occasions, a marquess on five, an earl on fourteen (although strictly speaking Sir Alec Douglas-Home renounced his title before taking it on), a viscount on five and a baron once.

    The Woolsacks on which the Lord Speaker and senior judges sit are large red cushions overstuffed with wool. The tradition dates back to the fourteenth century when wool formed a vital part of the national economy, but these days much of the stuffing comes from sheep in the Commonwealth.

BEHIND THE TITLE

- Seventy-four dukedoms have been created in the peerage of England, including six on one day (29 September 1397) and two for duchesses in their own right. Fully half are now extinct, the most recent to go being the last Duke of Leeds who died unmarried in 1964, and five of the survivors are directly descended from Charles II's illegitimate sons.

  Sir Winston Churchill is the only person known to have refused a dukedom, supposedly turning down both London and Dover in order not to compromise the political career of his son, Randolph.

- Traditionally, marquesses had estates on the marches, or borders, of the country. With responsibility for repelling invaders, the title was thus positioned above earls or counts with estates in inland counties.

  Despite the unusual feminine ending of the word, the only woman ever made a marquess in her own right was Anne Boleyn, in 1532, ahead of her marriage to Henry VIII.

  Viceroys of India were traditionally made marquesses when they retired from office, thus outranking prime ministers, who were rarely offered anything higher than an earldom.

- The word earl is far older, Anglo-Saxon, and is a derivation of *jarl*, Viking for chieftain. The equivalent of a continental count, historically they were responsible to the Crown for collecting fines and taxes. For this, earls were permitted to pocket every third penny they collected.

- The title viscount – from *viscomte*, literally vice- or deputy count – was introduced by a Frenchified Henry VI in the 1400s but is still treated with suspicion. There are relatively few viscounts, and most are only subsidiary titles used by the sons of marquesses and earls.

The oldest surviving viscountcy was created in 1550 and its holder, Lord Hereford, is an auctioneer. The last was created for a Labour Speaker of the House of Commons in 1983, but done so in the knowledge that as an unmarried seventy-four-year-old homosexual he was unlikely to produce an heir.

The title of baron, the lowest rank in the peerage of England, was introduced by William the Conqueror to recognize and reward loyalty. Fewer than one hundred survive from before the Civil War and of these the oldest still surviving is the thirteenth-century Barony de Ros. An English title given to a Scotsman, it has the unusual distinction that it can be held by a woman (and at the time of writing, it is).

As for so-called life peers, they're not aristocrats and so have no place in this chapter. In the 1950s when they began to flood into the Upper Chamber they were referred to by proper peers as the 'day boys'.

ENGLAND'S LONG-LOST LORD

Seventh Earl of Lucan

Dead or alive, but still very much this country's most famous fugitive, Richard John Bingham went on the run in November 1974 and cannot reliably be said to have been seen since. The peer fled after murdering the nanny at his Belgravia home, probably after mistaking her for his wife. When a bloodstained car was found at Newhaven, it seemed most likely Lucan had fled across the Channel or thrown himself into it. But no body has ever been found, so rumours persist that he was helped to escape by rich and influential friends.

Second Baron Moynihan

Following spells in the Coldstream Guards and playing the banjo in a Sydney nightclub, Anthony Moynihan was employed as a brothel-keeper, pimp, supergrass and drug-smuggler before converting to Islam and marrying a belly-dancer. His appearances in the House of Lords were mercifully rare; on one occasion it was requested that 'the noble lord sit down. He has bored us stiff for nearly three-quarters of an hour.' Fleeing the country after attempting to buy a Rolls-Royce with a dud cheque, he threatened to resume his seat as a Labour peer but happily died before he was able.

Fourth Earl Ferrers

The last peer to be hanged, Ferrers was dispatched in 1760 using a rope of common hemp (not silk, as is commonly supposed to be a nobleman's right). Earlier that year his lordship had been visited by a servant, to discuss rents on the family estate at Staunton Harold in Leicestershire. He shot him dead, and reflecting on the huge crowds at Tyburn his prophetic last words were: 'I suppose they never saw a lord hanged, and perhaps they will never see another.'

Sir Ralph de Standish

In June 1341, when revolting peasants marched on the City of London from Essex and Kent, talks were arranged at Smithfield between peasant leader Wat Tyler and Richard II. Things quickly went awry, however, with the Lord Mayor, William Walworth, drawing his sword and wounding Tyler in the neck. Seeking to defend the fourteen-year-old king, de Standish quickly moved in, stabbing Tyler to death with a short dagger. The red dagger can still be seen in the City of London's coat of arms today, and in a display case in Fishmongers' Hall.

Ninth Baron Dacre

Thomas Fiennes, Lord Dacre, inherited his grandfather's title and Herstmonceux Castle in Sussex and was a member of the jury at the trial of Anne Boleyn. In 1541, in the company of friends, he went poaching and was charged with murder after an affray, which left John Busbrig fatally wounded. Dacre and his pals were charged with murder, his Lordship being persuaded to plead guilty and throw himself on the mercy of the King. He did so, but the sovereign's mercy only went so far: whilst his co-accused were beheaded, he was taken to Tyburn and according to a witness 'strangled as common murderers are'.

Lord Gordon Gordon

Though only indirectly responsible for the 800 deaths which occurred during the anti-Catholic Gordon Riots of 1780, as their instigator the twenty-nine-year-old duke's son did well to escape being indicted for high treason. Nearly thirty of his supporters were sentenced to death but he spent just eight months in prison. Whilst incarcerated he learned to play the bagpipes, and frequently entertained six to eight guests to dinner in his cell.

Duke of Manchester

The original Dukes of Hazard, the eighth Duke was bankrupt before he was forty, the ninth spent time in Wormwood Scrubs after illegally pawning the family jewels, and after a surprise acquittal at the Old Bailey the twelfth was then jailed in the US (where he worked as a ski instructor) for his involvement in a second unsuccessful financial fraud. More recently, the thirteenth has served nine months in an Australian jail for obtaining money by deception.

MORE MONEY THAN SENSE

Fifth Marquess of Anglesey

When he died aged forty in 1905, 'Toppy' Anglesey was reckoned to have spent the sum equivalent today of half a billion pounds on elaborate jewelled costumes, a private theatre where he took the lead role in everything, and a car with perfumed exhaust pipes and a Louis XV ceiling. He'd been rich but not that rich, and in an attempt to clear his massive debts the family arranged a forty-day auction with 17,000 items going under the hammer. Bidding for his poodles started at a shilling each, and at the sale's conclusion all the paperwork was burned by a family desperate to put the whole sorry saga behind them.

Hon. Charles Hamilton

In the 1730s, Hamilton spent the entirety of a not inconsiderable inheritance building Painshill, England's first landscaped park. Items of expenditure included £700 for anyone prepared to dress like a hermit and live for a year in a cave (no one did) and more than a dozen beautiful follies. By the time he'd paid to move hills, excavate valleys and dig a 19-acre lake near where the A3 now crosses the M25, Hamilton had nothing left to build a house. Forced to sell the estate at a huge loss, he moved to Bath and died.

'BEWARE OF THE AGAPANTHUS'

Sign at the Faringdon, Oxfordshire, house of the fourteenth
Baron Berners

A good deal too unmarried for some of his more conventionally minded neighbours, between the wars the diplomat and opera and ballet music composer Gerald Hugh Tyrwhitt-Wilson (1883–1950) committed his life to colourful eccentricity. He was widely portrayed in novels and biographies, most notably as Lord Merlin in Nancy Mitford's *The Pursuit of Love* (1945). Berners' Rolls-Royce contained a clavichord keyboard, and he liked to drive around his estate wearing a pig's-head mask. He often dressed his dogs in diamonds and pearls and had his pigeons and even his meals dyed to match his moods – which more often than not were pink. The epitaph on his gravestone took a similarly light tone:

> Here lies Lord Berners
> One of the learners
> His great love of learning
> May earn him a burning
> But, Praise the Lord!
> He seldom was bored.

Tenth Duke of Manchester

In 1950, His Grace sold his seat, the fifty-bedroom Kimbolton Castle, all the land that went with it, the Holbeins, the Van Dycks and a spectacular 13,000-volume library – much of which had been in the family for nearly 350 years. The proceeds he invested in various African adventures, and by the time he died there was barely £70,000 left.

Sir John Bland Bt

Playing cards with chums at his London club, the Yorkshire baronet blew £32,000 in a single sitting – this was in 1755 so £32 *million* is probably nearer the mark today – before catching a boat across to France and shooting himself in the head.

Third Earl of Clarendon

The governor of a pre-independence New York, Clarendon decided that as the representative of a woman (Queen Anne) he should dress like one. In 1702 he appeared at the New York Assembly wearing a blue silk gown and blue satin shoes and, finding he liked it, he was soon spending so much on fans, hooped gowns and other finery that there was nothing left for his wife. She took to stealing in order to clothe herself and, with a major scandal brewing, the pair were soon recalled to England.

10

Fighting England

'How beautifully the English fight.'

Napoleon Bonaparte (1769–1821),
at the Battle of Waterloo

ALL VIOLENT ON THE WESTERN FRONT – WORLD WAR I IN NUMBERS

🔹 Of more than 10 million military war dead, the last man killed on the battlefield is thought to be Private George Edwin Ellison. After four years on the Western Front he had the tragic misfortune to be shot dead nearly five hours after the Armistice was signed.

🔹 Troops had legally to be nineteen years old in order to serve overseas, but approximately 250,000 managed to sneak across under-age. At least one of them (Sidney Lewis) was not even a teenager, and the first English soldier to be shot dead – Londoner Alan Parr – was only seventeen.

- Everybody likes to think that a privileged officer caste kept itself out of danger and that medical orderlies weren't proper soldiers. In fact, life expectancy among both officers and stretcher-bearers in the trenches was even less than the usual six-week average.

- At the Battle of Mons in 1914 the British rate of fire had been so rapid – at around thirty rounds per minute per man – that the Germans mistook their Lee-Enfield rifles for machine guns.

- Germany won the famous No Man's Land football match on Christmas Day, 1914. The score was 3–2.

- King's Regulations allowed for something called Field Punishment No. 1, in which offenders could be tied to a post occasionally within sight of German snipers. The sentence was handed down 60,210 times before being banned.

- Of the army's nearly 1 million horses, dead ones were frequently rendered for fat, which could then be used to make new explosives.

- England shipped 25 million tons of supplies to the Western Front, equivalent to 1,000 tons per mile of trench. The cost was horrendous and in September 1918, nearly £4 million worth of bullets were fired over a twenty-four-hour period.

- The target speed for the first tanks was only 4 mph. The word 'tank' was meaningless in this context, and intended only as code to prevent Germany finding out about Britain's new secret weapon.

- In an early attack using chlorine, German troops are thought to have killed 140 English officers in a single action. Until the invention by Edward Harrison of a practical gas mask, soldiers attempted to protect themselves by breathing through a piece of cloth soaked in their own urine.

- High above the trenches Manfred von Richthofen, aka the Red Baron, downed eighty Allied aircraft before being shot and killed. This compares to the sixty-one enemy planes shot down by the leading English ace, Major Edward Mannock VC, DSO, known as Mick, who also died in action.

- By the time the troops were demobbed and sent home, the Great War was estimated to have cost taxpayers in Britain around £9 billion at 1918 values. The other thing that happened when the troops were demobbed, or rather nine months later, was that the birth-rate increased by almost 50 per cent.

FROM TROPHY TO TRIUMPH

By far the best-loved weapon ever produced in England, and without doubt one of the most effective, for all its lethal genius the Spitfire drew its DNA not from a machine built to fight but rather one meant to win races.

Indeed, as the first machine ever to exceed 400 mph on land, sea or air, the Supermarine S6 seaplane was created to win just one race: the Schneider Trophy.

ରଚ ରଚ ରଚ

The single most prestigious flying event of the inter-war period, for almost two decades and before crowds of up to a million, the Schneider Trophy pitted French against English and Italian against American. For a while it even looked like a well-matched fight, until 1931 when England was handed the trophy for keeps after winning three years in succession.

∞ ∞ ∞

Designed by Reginald Mitchell, the aircraft which achieved this extraordinary feat boasted a staggering 2,600 horsepower courtesy of its supercharged Rolls-Royce R-Type V-12 engine. This had been sketched out in the sand by Sir Henry Royce while he was walking on the beach at West Wittering, and uniquely went on to break the land, water and air speed records.

∞ ∞ ∞

Just as the S6 evolved into the most famous fighter plane of its era, so this same engine rapidly morphed into the celebrated Merlin. Capable of seemingly endless development, the pair went on to fight together on almost every front and – as the only Allied fighter to remain in production for the entire war – the Spitfire was still in service in the 1950s, nearly thirty years after its illustrious ancestor first took to the air.

ALL THIS AND WORLD WAR, TOO: WEAPONS WHICH SEEMED A GOOD IDEA AT THE TIME

In an attempt to smash through Hitler's coastal defences ahead of D-Day, boffins at the Admiralty Directorate of Miscellaneous Weapon Development – aka the Wheezers and Dodgers – devised the Great Panjandrum. This was designed to deliver nearly 2 tonnes of high explosives across the English Channel without endangering Allied personnel.

᠗ ᠗ ᠗

Unfortunately, the Panjandrum, which was essentially a huge bomb slung between two rocket-powered wheels, lost its bearings on its first outing in 1943 and ran amok. More rockets were fitted to a second bomb to cure the problem, but this too spun round before toppling over and almost killing a cameraman who was on hand to record the results.

᠗ ᠗ ᠗

HMS *Persil* was the nickname of another initiative from the Wheezers and Dodgers, a cunning plan to prevent English lakes, rivers and reservoirs from being used as informal navigational aids by German aircrews. The idea was to spread a film of coal dust on the water's surface, making it look more like land when viewed from the air. As well as the plan's obvious environmental deficit, when tested on the River Thames it was found that the slightest breeze or tidal drift meant the dust would quickly collect by the water's edge. To make matters worse, it was occasionally mistaken for solid tarmac by pedestrians walking in the blackout.

᠗ ᠗ ᠗

Famous Wheezer recruits included the novelist Nevil Shute and Barnes 'Bouncing Bomb' Wallis, although neither of these two is to be held responsible for the ill-fated Hajile scheme. This was conceived to deliver *materiel* using rocket-powered platforms instead of parachutes, which had a tendency to drift off-target as well as attracting enemy fire as they made their slow descent. Unfortunately Hajile also had a tendency to spiral out of control at the first possible opportunity.

᠗ ᠗ ᠗

The name was coined after a prototype demolished the Wheezers' own engineering shed, Hajile being Elijah in reverse, a reference to the Biblical prophet who went up to heaven in a fiery chariot.

The Unrotated Projectile was a complex anti-aircraft weapon comprising short-range rockets fitted with long trailing wires and miniature parachutes. These were fired like a curtain ahead of approaching aircraft, the idea being to create what was in effect an aerial minefield. Becoming snagged on one of the wires the enemy pilot could not avoid pulling the explosive rocket towards him which would then explode destroying his aircraft.

If the wind turned, this same drifting ordnance risked detonating on contact with the very people launching it, hence its prompt withdrawal from service.

∞ ∞ ∞

America may have pioneered bat bombs and the pigeon-guided missile, and Soviet Russia the anti-tank dog, but the exploding rat was England's own. In an initiative launched by the Special Operations Executive (see Chapter 6: Secret England), dead rats were stuffed with high explosive, then secreted in coal supplies in the hope that they would disable German coal-fired boilers.

∞ ∞ ∞

The Germans found one before it could do any damage, although it has since been claimed that so much time was then wasted looking for more of them that the original aim of disrupting weapons manufacture was to some degree achieved.

∞ ∞ ∞

With aluminium and steel in such short supply in 1940s England, Admiralty adviser Geoffrey Pyke hatched a plan to build aircraft carriers and giant battleships using a combination of ice and sawdust.

∞ ∞ ∞

With characteristic modesty Pyke dubbed the mixture 'pykrete' and using a 1000 tonne scale model was able to demonstrate its impressive resistance to both shells and torpedoes.

∞ ∞ ∞

Being 86 per cent frozen water, each of these vessels needed to be fitted with a vast refrigeration plant and 10,000 tonnes of steel pipework to ensure its rigidity – a material which was also in short supply.

ഔ ഔ ഔ

Less a weapon and more a means of defence, Kent's Acoustic Mirrors (known locally as 'the listening ears') are spectacular concrete relics of a pre-radar world. They were intended to provide early warnings of enemy aircraft – fixed-wing as well as inflatable – by amplifying the sound of their engines as they approached over the English Channel.

ഔ ഔ ഔ

The three survivors of 'the listening ears' at Denge worked crudely and only up to a point, as the development of faster aircraft meant that the bombs were soon falling before anyone even realized they were on their way.

ഔ ഔ ഔ

A planned network of 'listening ears' stretching around the south and east coasts was never completed, but another survivor can be seen at Kilnsea in Yorkshire's East Riding.

ഔ ഔ ഔ

Briefly the world's fastest aeroplane, the 1946 De Havilland DH.108 was the first in this country to exceed the speed of sound. All three prototypes of the Havilland DH. 108 crashed, killing their pilots. The first loss was at mach 0.9 when a structural failure caused the wings to collapse, killing Geoffrey de Havilland Jr. A second pilot died following a faulty oxygen supply, and the third stalled, prompting the pilot to bail but at such low altitude that his parachute had no time to open.

GONE AND FORGOTTEN

The largest ever influx of wartime refugees into England wasn't Jews fleeing Hitler's death camps, exiled Poles, nor Charles de Gaulle's Free French. It wasn't even during World War II, but at the start of the First, when more than 250,000 Belgians made their way across the North Sea. At one point they were arriving at a rate of up to 16,000 a day, yet when they returned home they went almost without leaving a trace.

∾ ∾ ∾

The English were mostly happy to see these refugees, and when it became apparent they'd be here for a while many thousands moved into purpose-built villages dotted around the country.

∾ ∾ ∾

Elisabethville, named after their own queen, was a little bit of sovereign Belgian territory in Birtley, Tyne and Wear, with Belgian schools, shops, churches, hospitals and even prisons and currency. English visitors required a special pass to enter by the all-Belgian *gendarmerie* manning the gates.

∾ ∾ ∾

With the exception of a modest monument given in thanks by the Belgian government in London's Embankment Gardens, one is hard pressed to find anything to show that for several years England was home to literally hundreds of thousands of Belgians.

∾ ∾ ∾

Whitehall was initially as pleased as everyone else to have so many 'plucky' Belgians here, but the minute the Kaiser was beaten, with so many tens of thousands of returning British soldiers needing to be housed, the government was keen to wave the Belgian refugees off.

Belgium wanted the refugees back to begin rebuilding their country. Belgians found their jobs terminated, their livelihoods gone, and with no money had no choice but to return home immediately. One of the few positives was free ferry tickets – but these were strictly one-way and time-limited.

∞ ∞ ∞

Within a year at least 230,000 Belgians had sailed home. Most of the others followed shortly afterwards, and a hundred years later just two buildings remain at Elisabethville. Today, for most English people, the name doesn't even ring a bell.

A FAR DEADLIER GAME

Soon after the start of the Hitler offensive, renowned games-and toymaker John Jaques IV (see Chapter 5, Sporting England) was contacted by a representative of MI9, the top-secret department for what was termed 'Escape and Evasion'.

∞ ∞ ∞

The function of MI9 was to assist downed aircrews and escaped prisoners of war attempting to make it back to England. Working closely with Jaques, the department's Major Christopher Clayton Hutton devised numerous toys and games of a sort never seen before. Intended to be sent to PoWs and others who, under the terms of the 1929 Geneva Convention, were allowed to correspond with their families, they cleverly concealed gadgets likely to be of use to anyone attempting to make a break-out.

∞ ∞ ∞

Some of the devices included maps secreted between the card layers of Ludo and Snakes and Ladders boards, banknotes hidden in the wooden awls used to lace Jaques' famous leather footballs, and even miniature compasses buried in the tops of the pegs used to play Deck Quoits.

Such devices, life-saving tools dressed up as playthings, enabled more than 35,000 members of the home and Commonwealth forces to find their way back from enemy territory.

ഔ ഔ ഔ

Other companies were involved too – the green Cumberland Pencil contained the smallest compass ever made and rolled-up route maps where the lead would normally be.

Jaques HQ still have a cherished souvenir of their covert wartime contribution. This is an old-fashioned cribbage board which opens to reveal a long, slim panel carved to conceal a useful MI9 accessory: a hacksaw blade.

'DR BRIGHTON'

This cheery nickname was given to what was without doubt England's most exotic military hospital. It was created when Brighton's Royal Pavilion was remodelled as a 720-bed hospital specifically for the more than 1.5 million Imperial Indian Army troops who took part in the Great War.

ഔ ഔ ഔ

With its treasures removed, and the curtains and carpets replaced by more practical blinds and linoleum, the famous onion dome became an operating theatre while the King's Music Room, Ballroom and South Drawing Room were all hastily converted into wards.

ഔ ഔ ഔ

The first patients arrived in December 1914, suffering from 'trench back' as well as the inevitable shot and shrapnel injuries and – later – gas.

ഔ ഔ ഔ

To boost morale the patients were encouraged to believe that their King-Emperor George V had vacated his palace in order to accommodate them. In fact, Queen Victoria, never a fan of Brighton with what she saw as its regrettable appeal to cockney daytrippers, had long sold it to the local council for £53,000.

෨ ෨ ෨

With the experience of the Indian Mutiny still fresh in military minds, there were many sensitivities to be observed. No beef or pork was allowed in the grounds. Separate kitchens and even taps were provided for the different cohorts of Sikhs, Hindus and Muslims, and special ingredients were obtained to prepare authentic dal and chapattis.

෨ ෨ ෨

The authorities were also careful to acknowledge the niceties of India's traditional caste system when it came to organizing staff on the various wards. Dalits or 'Untouchables' were strictly segregated, and no one was knowingly treated by a member of an inappropriate or lower caste.

෨ ෨ ෨

Among the patients was Jemadar Mir Dast, a member of 57th Wilde's Rifles, who was gassed at Ypres and later photographed being awarded the Victoria Cross by the King. This and other propaganda-boosting images sold in huge numbers throughout the Empire.

෨ ෨ ෨

A book about the restorative effects of 'Dr Brighton' was translated into Urdu and Gurmukkhi in order to persuade others in the sub-continent to enlist.

11

Building England

*'Domus sua cuique est tutissimum refugium.' Meaning,
roughly, that an Englishman's home is his castle.*

Sir Edward Coke, jurist, 1628

From its very oldest building to one of the newest – from
Wiltshire's 5,700-year-old West Kennet long barrow to
London's opinion-dividing Shard, then – England's single-
minded approach to architecture has left us a legacy which
includes some of the most remarkable, strangest and most
engaging constructions anywhere in Europe.

■ ■ ■

654: A contender for England's oldest church, St Peter's-
on-the-Wall at Bradwell-juxta-Mare, Essex, was built by
St Cedd. Saxon, and using recycled Roman materials, the
barn-like chapel straddles the 160-metre outer wall of
Othona, a fort built to defend Rome's Saxon shore.

1176: London Bridge, the first stone bridge across the Thames, was built by Peter of Colechurch and survived for more than 600 years. Amazingly, a much earlier Roman bridge provided the support for it, as well as several Saxon predecessors. In fact, these original Roman piers continued to underpin every new bridge until Sir John Rennie's 'New London Bridge' of 1831.

■ ■ ■

1230: England's oldest royal effigy, King John's, lies in its most unlucky cathedral. Worcester Cathedral collapsed in 1175 and in 1203, when the restoration was complete, it caught fire. At the next attempt to rebuild (in 1348), the Black Death swept across Europe, killing half the workforce. Somehow it was completed and in 1502 the despised king's effigy at last found a companion in the almost unknown Prince Arthur, who died young, leaving the throne to his brother Henry VIII.

■ ■ ■

1280: With the completion of its spire, Lincoln Cathedral became the first building in the world to top the nearly 4,000-year-old Great Pyramid of Giza, at 525 feet. What's more, had it not been destroyed in a storm in 1549, the spire would have remained the tallest building on earth until 1884, when the Washington Monument was completed.

■ ■ ■

1362: The spire of St Mary and All Saints at Chesterfield in Derbyshire leans slightly but twists dramatically, through more than 45 degrees. Locally, they blame the Devil, but structural engineers are more inclined towards the theory that its builders provided insufficient bracing for more than 30 tonnes of lead used to cover it. The heat of the sun causes this to expand more on one side than the other, leading over time to the attractive deformation we see today.

1456: One of England's largest houses, Knole in Kent is a so-called 'calendar house' having at one point boasted 365 rooms, 52 staircases, twelve entrances and seven courtyards. Avon Tyrrell House in Hampshire was another with 365 windows, 52 rooms, twelve chimneys, four wings (one for each season) and seven external doors. It was reportedly built with the winnings of an 1882 bet that the owner could buy, train and ride a Grand National winner: in heavy snow 'Seaman' won, but never raced again and is buried in the grounds.

■ ■ ■

1613: An early health and safety nightmare, the original Globe Theatre in Southwark took only an hour to burn right down to the ground.

■ ■ ■

1725: A classic Palladian house set in a magnificent landscaped grounds, Stourhead in Wiltshire was built for the banker Henry Hoare and later reproduced in miniature as the country estate of Lady Penelope Creighton-Ward of *Thunderbirds* fame.

■ ■ ■

1734: Almost unknown outside Derby – it doesn't even have its own Wikipedia page – Bennetts of Irongate is the oldest department store anywhere in the world. It still trades from the original building.

■ ■ ■

1772: The widest private house in England is Yorkshire's eighteenth-century Wentworth Woodhouse, at a staggering 180 metres. It has well over 300 rooms spread over 23,000 square metres – but almost no land.

■ ■ ■

1830: Not far shy of 2,200 metres in length, everyone knows that the pier at Southend-on-Sea is the world's longest. Not so well known is that it was taken over by the Royal Navy during World War II and renamed HMS *Leigh*.

■ ■ ■

1843: The day before a statue of the great man was winched into place atop London's Nelson Column, fourteen people sat down to a windswept meal served on a constructed platform at the very summit, in what might be considered one of the earliest pop-up restaurants.

■ ■ ■

1864: England's only inland lighthouse was built in east London for experimenting with new technology for lighthouses and lightships. Since New Year's Day 2000 it has hosted *Long Player*, a bizarre piece for Tibetan singing bowls, which at 1,000 years' duration is the longest composition in musical history.

■ ■ ■

1871: When it opened, the new Royal Albert Hall was lit entirely by gas-burners. It was possible to light all 11,000 jets in just ten seconds, and Eau de Cologne supplied by M. Rimmel was pumped through the ventilation to sweeten the atmosphere inside.

■ ■ ■

1877: Lord Braybrooke, owner of Audley End in Essex, insisted that the tunnel portals for the Great Eastern Railway service running across his estate be in keeping with his great Jacobean palace. They remain the most ornate portals anywhere in England.

■ ■ ■

1879: Following an Act of Parliament permitting the destruction of an entire community to make way for Thirlmere reservoir, a modest whitewashed church is all that remains of the drowned Cumbria village of Wythburn.

■ ■ ■

1882: Tower Bungalows at Birchington-on-Sea in Kent was the first development anywhere of this kind of single-storey dwelling. Although nothing could be more English than a seaside bungalow, the name is actually derived from the Gujarati *baṅgalo* or Hindi *baṅglā*, meaning 'Bengali-style'.

■ ■ ■

1905: Built with a donation from an eccentric fossil-hunting baronet, at 110 metres, the University of Birmingham's Joseph Chamberlain Memorial Clock Tower was the tallest freestanding clock in the world. After more than a hundred years it still is, and students are traditionally advised against walking beneath it when the bells chime, for fear of failing their finals.

■ ■ ■

1910: Newquay's 'House in the Sea' is the only home in England to be on its own island and reached by a suspension bridge. Once home to Sir Arthur Conan Doyle (and the inventor of the 'igniter', an early form of spark plug) it can be rented for £6,000 a week.

■ ■ ■

1915: Stonehenge was sold to Mr Cecil Chubb who paid only £6,500 for it before donating it to the nation, possibly because his wife didn't like it. Contrary to popular belief, the world-famous prehistoric monument actually predates the Druids by at least a thousand years.

■ ■ ■

1920: What is thought to be the only thatched Tudor-style bus-stop, dovecot and weathervane in England was built as a memorial to the men of Westcott in Surrey who were lost in the Great War.

■ ■ ■

1937: A keen pilot but poor navigator, Mary Duchess of Bedford had the words 'Woburn Abbey' painted in large capital letters on the roof of her husband's ancestral home. Sadly, the seventy-one-year-old disappeared during a flight over the North Sea and her body was never recovered. The sign later caused some awkwardness when the house was occupied during the war by female naval personnel engaged in top-secret cipher work.

■ ■ ■

1946: No one's ever heard of it but the tallest building in England is a radio mast in Cumbria. At 365 metres, it is nearly 20 per cent taller than the Shard and forms part of the Skelton transmitting station, once the largest and most powerful shortwave station anywhere in the world.

■ ■ ■

1956: It took this long before England's last remaining human troglodyte or cave dweller moved into more conventional accommodation. At Holy Austin Rock in Staffordshire, cut into the face of Kinver Edge, the dwelling in question dates from around 1600, despite its Victorian appearance. At one time, a whole warren of similar houses provided accommodation on three levels for up to a dozen families. Apparently comfortable – cool in summer and relatively warm in the winter months – the last to survive is now owned by the National Trust.

■ ■ ■

1981: For nearly two decades, the longest single-span in the world, the Humber Bridge links Yorkshire and Lincolnshire and is so large that its two towers splay out at the top to take account of the curvature of the earth. Despite consuming 480,000 tonnes of concrete (and enough supporting cable to circle the equator twice), the bridge still flexes in the middle by nearly 3 metres.

■ ■ ■

1994: When the two halves of the Channel Tunnel linked up it was discovered that, rather than meeting halfway, the English diggers had made greater headway than the French. Eleven massive boring machines had been used to excavate the tunnels, one of which was later sold on eBay for £39,999.

■ ■ ■

2006: Just ten of England's fifty tallest buildings are outside London. Of these Beetham Tower in Manchester is the tallest (it is visible from ten counties) and has since been identified as the source of a mysterious hum which can be heard several hundred metres away. Worse in windy weather, the forty-seven-storey block caused problems for Granada Television, who claimed the hum was even bugging viewers of *Coronation Street*.

■ ■ ■

2008: Whilst being restored, Dorset's Clavell Tower, a Tuscan-style folly built in 1830 and used as a romantic getaway by Thomas Hardy, was moved 25 metres inland to prevent it falling off the eroding cliffs of the Jurassic Coast.

12

Educating England

'The dons of Oxford and Cambridge are too busy educating the young men to be able to teach them anything.'

Samuel Butler (1835–1902), author

THE LIGHT BLUES

Christ's College

One of just five Oxbridge colleges to have a swimming pool, Christ's is the oldest, believed to date back to the mid-seventeenth century.

Churchill College

In 1961, Nobel laureate Francis Crick resigned his fellowship on hearing the college was to get a chapel. He sent a cheque for ten guineas (£10.50) in the hope that college authorities would change their minds and build a brothel instead.

Corpus Christi College

For several hundred years, all teaching was in Latin and undergraduates were expressly forbidden to speak English within the college precincts.

Emmanuel College

In 2006, the college chapel became the first Church of England establishment to permit same-sex marriages.

Gonville and Caius College

Founded by Gonville (a vicar) the college was rescued by Caius (a physician) who provided the money needed to keep it running on condition that no Welshmen were admitted as undergraduates.

King's College

For many years students were recruited only from Eton and didn't need to pass any exams to be awarded bachelor's degrees.

Newnham College

The college boasts Europe's longest continuous corridor so that mid-nineteenth-century students shouldn't soil their petticoats by having to step outside.

Peterhouse

For decades, Cambridge was a famously good source of spies and double-agents. At the time of writing, the college's Master is Sir Richard Dearlove, erstwhile head of MI6.

Pembroke

Old-fashioned Pembroke still insists students dine wearing gowns yet was the first college to adopt newfangled electric lights in the 1880s.

Queens' College

Queens' produced its own postage stamps until 1886 when it was told by the General Post Office that to continue doing so would be illegal.

Sidney Sussex College

Oliver Cromwell's head is buried beneath the chapel even though he failed to graduate.

St Edmund's College

Until 1996 the college was refused admission to the university because its undergraduates were all Catholic.

Trinity College

Trinity has famously won more Nobel prizes than the whole of Africa.

Wolfson College

The floor of the main entrance hall is of granite recycled from the old London Bridge before the rest of it was shipped off to be rebuilt in Arizona.

THE DARK BLUES

Brasenose College

The curious name is thought to derive from a nose-shaped *brazen* (brass) doorknocker on a building which occupied the site before the college's foundation in 1509.

Christ Church

Christ Church has educated thirteen British prime ministers, only two fewer than the entire University of Cambridge.

Corpus Christi College

Since 1974 the Corpus Christi Tortoise Fair has included a race for any tortoises residing in Oxford colleges.

Exeter College

Exeter admitted Catholics in the seventeenth century but they were not allowed to graduate.

Jesus College

With only one exception the college appointed Welsh masters between 1571 and 1915 and its undergraduate magazine is called *The Sheepshagger*.

Keble College

Keble's Victorian Gothic building was reportedly so unpopular in the 1880s that a secret society was formed in which prospective candidates for membership were required to steal bricks from the building in the hope that it would eventually collapse.

Lincoln College

On Ascension Day, a door connecting Lincoln with Brasenose is opened and members of the latter are invited to join the men of Lincoln for a free beer at lunchtime. However, the beer is flavoured with ivy to discourage anyone from drinking more than his share.

Mansfield College

Uniquely the chapel at Mansfield has never been consecrated.

Merton College

Merton was the only college to side with the Roundheads during the English Civil War.

Pembroke College

Pembroke's student society or JCR bought a Francis Bacon painting in 1953 for £150 and sold it for £400,000 forty years later.

St Anne's College

To the delight of pub quiz masters, throughout its long years as a women-only college the mascot of St Anne's has been a beaver.

St Catherine's College

'St Catz' is one of very few twentieth-century buildings to be Grade-I listed, its Danish architect Arne Jacobsen having also designed all the furniture, lampshades and cutlery.

University College

Grace, which is read in Latin before formal meals three times a week, is so long that even the Master and Senior Fellows are not expected to memorize it.

Wadham College

Since the 1980s all student functions conclude with the playing of *Free Nelson Mandela*, a song written by Coventry musician Jerry Dammers. Mandela himself visited the college in 1997.

13

Celebrating England

'The first of April is the day we remember what we are the other three hundred and sixty-four days of the year.'

Mark Twain (1835–1910), author and humorist

JANUARY

Maldon Mud Race, Essex

In an east coast variation of the inland sport of bog-snorkelling, some 250 competitors engage in an unholy struggle through the stinking greeny-black mud of the Blackwater Estuary. The winner, traditionally of either sex, is the person with the most up-to-date tetanus jab. The losers are those who forgot to gaffer-tape their trainers to their ankles. The temperature is of course bitterly cold, prompting postponement to April or May in some years.

The Haxey Hood, Haxey, Lincolnshire

Locals compete to become 'Lord of the Hood' in a stagey re-enactment of a 700-year-old tradition which began when the elegant Lady de Mowbray was out riding. According to tradition she lost her hat to a gust of wind and a gaggle of farm labourers set out to retrieve it. The rest is history: the raucous sport of hat-hunting was born, with much drinking of ale and singing of traditional folk songs.

FEBRUARY

Football, Ashbourne, Derbyshire

Each Shrove Tuesday and Ash Wednesday, a variation of soccer is played in which the entire town becomes the pitch. Placing the goal mouths 3 miles apart, and as per the game's Elizabethan origins, those born on one side of the river play those born on the other, a goal being scored when the ball is tapped three times against a special marker board. It's not as rough as it used to be – participants no longer die – but savvy shopkeepers still board up their windows.

APRIL

Dwile Flonking, Lewes, Sussex

A relatively recent pursuit, regulars at the Lewes Arms pub take on members of the local opera society with players standing in a circle while flinging a dishcloth which has been soaked in stale beer at one another. It's your turn with the cloth after you've been hit in the face. (A variation of this is also played at the Dog Inn in Ludham Bridge, Norfolk.)

Maundy Thursday

The traditional giving of royal alms – specially struck coins which have a depressing habit of turning up on eBay the following weekend – commemorates the Last Supper. The arrangements are the responsibility of the Lord High Almoner, traditionally a senior bishop. He still wears a towel at his waist as a reminder to Christian kings to follow the example of Christ and to echo His humility in washing the feet of those present at the Last Supper. Elizabeth I was a great fan of this aspect, but concerns over the generally low standard of hygiene displayed by the masses meant that actual foot-washing came to an end during the reign of the more fastidious King George I in 1730.

MAY

Mayor-making, Rye, East Sussex

Thought to be unique to the ancient borough and Cinque Port, this annual event sees the newly installed mayor throwing pennies from the upper window of the Mayor's Parlour at the Town Hall to crowds of waiting children in Market Street below. The coins have to be hot in order to celebrate (if that's the word) a former Rye mayor who was also the town's Member of Parliament. He notoriously bribed voters using coins from Rye's own mint, arranging for these to be minted and put into circulation so rapidly that they were still hot to touch.

Worm Charming, Willaston, Cheshire

What the organizers insist is the World Championship, sees participants trying to perfect the ancient art of worm charming by encouraging little wrigglers to appear above ground. Incredibly, in the 2009 event one ten-year-old managed to charm 567 specimens up from the depths. A similar event is held in Devon, but it's been said that they cheat there by pouring cider onto the ground.

Cheese Rolling, Cooper's Hill, Gloucestershire

Attracting up to 15,000 spectators, and every year threatened by concerns about health and safety, the success of this annual event lies in observing the variety of ways in which competitors willingly risk wrist, leg, arm and ankle as they run, slip and slide down a 50 per cent gradient in pursuit of a large cheese disc. Sadly, even its keenest adherents realize that its geographical specificity means that it will almost certainly never be accepted by the International Olympic Committee.

The 'Obby 'Oss, Padstow, Cornwall

One of the few things in the town to have nothing to do with television cook Rick Stein, what some insist is the oldest dance festival in the country sees Padstow's inhabitants dancing around two pretend horses, one called 'Old' and the other 'Blue Ribbon'. All this takes place to the sound of drums and accordions. Its origins are thought to be Celtic, but latterly it won the support of the temperance movement, which saw it as a means of encouraging people to do something other than drink. This hasn't worked.

Hunting the Earl of Rone, Combe Martin, Devon

In one of the southwest's oldest and oddest customs, costumed characters flood the streets looking for the Earl of Rone. After four days – it always takes four days – they find him. The nobleman, based on a seventeenth-century Earl of Tyrone, is then paraded through the streets back-to-front on a donkey before being 'shot', knocked off and thrown into the sea. For nearly a 140 years the event was banned for the inevitable licentiousness and drunken behaviour, but since being revived in 1974 it has been generally orderly.

State Opening of Parliament, Westminster, London

Barges no longer provide the quickest and safest way to travel from Hampton Court Palace to Westminster – although the way things are going with traffic in London that could change – but the Monarchy likes to do things the traditional way. When the Crown Jewels – in this case the Imperial State Crown together with the Sword of State, the Cap of Maintenance and their bearers – travel by carriage to Parliament, they still do so under the protection of the Queen's Barge-master and her Royal Watermen. The regalia are also entitled to an escort made up of Household Cavalry troops, and receive a royal salute.

JUNE

The Bognor Birdman, Bognor Regis, Sussex

Each year since 1971, several human birdmen take a running jump off piers in this part of Sussex in order to see who can fly the furthest or, more precisely, hit the water last. Bizarre costumes and some astonishingly complex man-powered flying machines are lured to the coast by a prize of up to £30,000 for the longest flight over 100 metres. After initially strong competition from Germany, Ron Freeman has scooped the top prize no fewer than five times.

Egg throwing, Swaton, Lincolnshire

Swaton hosts a cracking annual eggstravaganza believed to date from as early as 1322. The event includes egg-catching, egg-and-spoon relays and machine-assisted egg-hurling – all of it for a good cause – and is said to commemorate a fourteenth-century cleric who kept chickens and would lob eggs over the River Eau to starving peasants.

World Stinging Nettle Eating Championship, Marshwood, Dorset

Hosted by the sixteenth-century Bottle Inn as part of the local beer festival, competitors consume *raw* nettle leaves as fast as possible. The competition is said to have begun with an argument between a couple of pub regulars about who had the tallest crop of nettles. The competition runs over an hour, at the end of which the winner is the person with the largest number of bare stalks. Twenty metres is not uncommon, and in 2014 a man from over the border in Devon managed twenty-four, to be crowned King of the Stingers before an estimated thousand spectators.

Yorkshire Pudding Boat Race, Brawby, North Yorkshire

Real Yorkshire puddings made of flour and eggs, but larger and coated with yacht varnish, compete to see which can be paddled across the perilous waters of Bob's Pond in this little Ryedale village.

World Toe Wrestling Championships, Ashbourne, Derbyshire

With opponents sitting opposite each other, bare-footed and digits locked together on the official 'toedium', the winner is the one able to manoeuvre his or her opponent's foot to the side of the frame. Now in its thirty-eighth year, the proceeds go to charity, and the event is definitely not for the ticklish.

JULY

Skipton Sheep Day, Skipton, Yorkshire

Unaccountably knocked off the 2014 fixture list by the Tour de France, this annual event sees sheep of all ages racing down the town's historic high street to celebrate its long farming heritage, while sheepdogs take a break from their normal tasks and engage in a once-a-year duck-herding contest.

Dunmow Flitch Trials, Great Dunmow, Essex

With a history stretching back around 900 years, these mock-judicial proceedings are mentioned both by Chaucer in *The Wife of Bath's Tale* and by William Langland in his *Vision of Piers Plowman*. Complete with wigs and gowns and with a flitch, or side, of bacon for the winning couple, the event takes place each leap year when young couples attempt to convince a jury of six maidens and six bachelors that they have neither been unfaithful nor exchanged a cross word with each other during the previous twelve months. Following criticism by a local noteworth who described it as 'an idle custom bringing people of indifferent character into the neighbourhood', the Flitch Trials were in danger of petering out in the mid-1800s, before being relaunched by an enthusiastic Victorian novelist.

AUGUST

Kettlewell Scarecrow Festival, Yorkshire

William and Kate, Ronnie Barker, Top Gear's Jeremy Clarkson, Abba and the Queen are just some of the well-known figures created in straw-stuffed effigy in this Yorkshire village each summer. With celebrities often treated with more wit than respect – the petrolhead presenter was recently shown in the stocks – the festival attracts large crowds of visitors leading to several imitations popping up around the country.

SEPTEMBER

The Great Wrekin Barrel Race, Shropshire

A bit like cheese rolling in reverse – only with a barrel, and no rolling allowed – the team event involves running up to the 407-metre summit of this Shropshire outcrop, while carrying a full 40-litre barrel (water rather than beer, in case of wastage). It's said to take fit men twenty minutes to reach the top, the idea being to commemorate the so-called Wrekin Wakes of the 1800s, when barrels of ale were hauled up the hill as part of boisterous local celebrations.

Gurning World Championship, Egremont, Cumbria

One of the oldest fairs in the country, the Egremont Crab Fair dates back to the mid-thirteenth century. No one's quite sure of the origins but ugly folk would come from miles around, attempting to make themselves uglier still by pulling ghastly faces whilst sticking their heads through a braffin, or horse-collar. OAPs have long seemed to hold the stage in this event, not so much because they have greater experience or ingenuity, but because warty skin, wrinkles and removable teeth can each be turned to excellent advantage.

The Horn Dance, Abbots Bromley, Staffordshire

Held on 'Wakes Monday' (the first Monday after the first Sunday after 4 September) the dance sees six Deer-men with reindeer antlers on their heads accompanied by Maid Marian (invariably a man in drag), a hobby-horse and a fool. Following a 10-mile course and stopping at a dozen places along the way, they are joined by musicians playing traditional tunes on an old-fashioned melodeon and a triangle. Supporters claim the ritual is nearly a thousand years old (although by that time English reindeer were already extinct) and Cromwell banned it, suggesting it must be quite fun.

OCTOBER

Conker World Championships, Ashton, Oundle, Northamptonshire

In danger of dying out, conker fighting seems to have been with us for ever, although horse chestnuts only arrived in England in the seventeenth century from Eastern Europe, and no reference to the game has been found which predates 1858. With separate events for ladies, gentlemen and juniors, the Ashton games have been run since the mid-1960s, since when more than £400,000 has been raised for charity. Various traditional niceties are still observed, including the practice of reciting 'Oddly oddly onker my first conker' upon finding the first fruit of the season.

Souling, Halton, Cheshire

For centuries, actors known as mummers have performed plays at the beginning of November, a tradition intended to protect villagers and their communities from outsiders and dark spirits. At Halton, a knight, Sir George, battles the Turkish Champion, with other characters making brief appearances such as Beelzebub, an old woman (traditionally a man in drag) and an inebriated medic. Similar festivities take place elsewhere in the county, at Chester, Antrobus, Comberbach and Warburton, with 'soul cakes' sometimes distributed among the audience at the play's conclusion.

Flaming Tar-Barrels, Ottery St Mary, Devon

For those killjoys anxious about schoolchildren injuring themselves with conkers on strings, the very thought of tar-barrel racing should be enough to drive them into the sea. An old custom believed to date back to the seventeenth century, this annual event sees the townspeople racing through the streets carrying wooden barrels of flaming hydrocarbons on their backs. Only those born locally are eligible and the idea is to exorcize demons, fumigate the ancient hovels of the poor, warn of the Armada, or possibly just to celebrate the capture of Guy Fawkes. No one's quite sure, or that bothered actually, as it pulls in a big crowd and is a lot of fun.

DECEMBER

Christmas has been with us for a while now, but many of its traditions are not quite what one might imagine.

෴ ෴ ෴

The first printed book of Christmas carols was produced by William Caxton's apprentice Wynkyn de Worde in 1521, but much of its meaning has been lost in the years since. Cheerful choruses of *Good King Wenceslas*, for example, rarely bring to mind St Stephen, the first Christian to die for his faith, who was brutally stoned to death on Boxing Day AD 30.

෴ ෴ ෴

Nor is pantomime quite the English pleasure many assume it to be. Its origins lie with Italy's old *Comedia dell'Arte*, brought to England by a dancing-master from Shrewsbury. John Weaver staged his first production at London's Lincoln's Inn Theatre in 1717, and it was a huge success despite a less than cheery title – *Harlequin Executed* – and the fact that the two principal characters, colourful Harlequin and Columbine, never actually got to speak. They were also meant to be invisible, which is probably why most companies now opt for seemingly endless adaptations of *Cinderella, Jack and the Beanstalk* and *Peter Pan*.

෴ ෴ ෴

The Christmas tree is also a relatively modern innovation that only arrived in Britain during the reign of Queen Victoria. Like the Royal Consort Prince Albert, it came from Germany, where it is popularly held to represent a young spruce tree offered in place of a child sacrifice to the old Norse god Odin. Traditional decorations of holly and green ivy suggest Saxon origins, although the seasonal popularity of mistletoe, supposedly the most sacred plant of the Druids, points to pagan rather than Christian roots.

The yule log is also an import, taking its name from the Icelandic *Jol*, another heathen festival which saw great seasoned logs brought into homes and laid across the hearth. These would be lit with great ceremony and left to burn while the festivities continued over the next day and night.

ഗൗ ഗൗ ഗൗ

In fact, the only truly English innovation is the Christmas card. The first appeared in 1844 and was sent by the artist and Royal Academician William Dobson. Sir Henry Cole started producing them commercially two years later but an attempt was made then to have them banned on moral grounds, because the illustration showed a family cheerfully imbibing glasses of wine.

14

Eccentric England

*'The amount of eccentricity in a society has
generally been proportional to the amount of genius,
mental vigour and moral courage it contained.
That so few now dare to be eccentric marks the chief
danger of the time.'*

John Stuart Mill (1806–73), philosopher,
civil servant and economist

The past, said L. P. Hartley in *The Go-Between*, is another
country, and looking back at England in 1946 who wouldn't
wish that it literally was? Bankrupted by the war, bombsites
and burned-out buildings everywhere you looked, and with
food rationing destined to remain on the menu for another
eight years, it was a long way from anyone's idea of a green
and pleasant land.

Anyone except Ben Sansum, at least, a thirty-something from Godmanchester in Cambridgeshire, who has surrounded himself with seventy-year-old music, seventy-year-old clothes, seventy-year-old austerity furniture and even pre-war carpets in a bid not so much to experience the 1940s as to actually live there. Sansum admits to having a modern fridge ('meat-safes aren't great these days'), but when he's home from his job as a British Airways steward his immersion is total. He cooks on an old range, wrings his clothes out using a very old mangle, and prefers a wind-up gramophone to anything from Spotify or Twitter. His dedication to the decade is such that his partner prefers to live instead in a normal house nearby, with all the usual mod cons.

In one sense at least there is nothing surprising here, for the words English and eccentric run together so naturally – quintessentially is another one – that we sometimes tend to think we have a monopoly on them in this country. If pressed, we might grudgingly acknowledge that a foreigner occasionally comes close – the French motor-car manufacturer Ettore Bugatti, for example, had his shoes made with separate compartments for his big toes – but we rarely celebrate them as we do Ben with his braces and boxes of Borax, and mostly think they're rather silly.

THE LIMPING LADIES

Sometimes fashion reaches a bit further than one might expect. Whether or not it's true that we leave one waistcoat button undone because the gourmandizing Edward VII was forced to do so, one of England's strangest ever fashions certainly developed from the public's determination to copy his wife's example.

When she married the future king, Alexandra had a scar on her neck which she concealed by wearing a choker, and a pronounced limp from a bout of rheumatic fever. The adoption of the choker by society ladies was not surprising: for centuries courtiers have aped kings in both manners and dress. Far more remarkable was that instead of politely ignoring Alexandra's limp, thousands of women actually started copying it.

Faking a limp takes practice and concentration, so impressionable women would wear odd shoes beneath their crinolines so their faltering steps appeared natural. It didn't take outfitters long to notice and, recognizing a potentially lucrative trend among 'the young, the capricious, the suggestible and the status-obsessed – or to put it another way, the fashionable', the more canny among them started to sell pairs of shoes with one high heel and one low.

Expense fortunately prevented the fashion from trickling too far down the classes and by 1869 the press were railing against a 'monstrosity . . . as painful as it is idiotic and ludicrous'. Underlining just how silly the whole thing was, a racehorse was named Alexandra Limp, and then, as quickly as it had begun, the fad was finished. The Princess was stuck with her disability, but the rest of society moved on.

THE DULL MEN'S CLUB

Nothing makes less sense than another man's hobby and, recognizing this, an organization now 5,000 members strong published a calendar in 2014 celebrating the activities of a dozen of its members.

JANUARY: Roundabout Photographer

Kevin Beresford from Redditch is the President of the UK Roundabout Appreciation Society and spends his weekends photographing particularly special examples.

FEBRUARY: Card Recycler

Ken McCoy from Leeds has sent his wife the same Valentine Card every year for nearly four decades. Not one that looks the same, but the same actual card.

NOW WASH YOUR HANDS

Concerned at the loss of some of this country's most historic lavatories – at least two have been converted into subterranean homes, others are now cafés, nightclubs and bars – Rachel Erikson of London Loo Tours has spent the best part of two years organizing guided visits around the best of them. Taking in Bloomsbury, Portobello and – inevitably – Waterloo, the visits began as a joke with Rachel herself scouting for a loo where she didn't need to pay to spend a penny.

Erikson took the plunge only after realizing just how much history and culture is bound up in the seemingly simple street *pissoir*. The treasures she has unearthed include marble counters, wonderful brass taps, urinals with little targets to improve the aim of gentleman users, and an authentic Thomas Crapper 'Venerable' model from the 1890s, which is still in use. Her knowledge about the subject would probably get her a PhD, but so far she has resisted the lure of academic respectability.

MARCH: Drain Spotter

Maintaining verges and ditches in his native Cumbria, the wonderfully named Archie Workman is fortunate enough to combine his trade with his hobby of spotting unusual drain covers and plotting the pipes which lie beneath.

APRIL: Gotta Lotta Bottle

Steve Wheeler from Malvern has spent more than thirty years amassing a collection of more than 20,000 milk bottles which are displayed in an 80-foot-long private museum in his garden.

MAY: Defending the Realm

Doing it the only way he knows how, seventy-three-year-old Michael Kennedy from Hunstanton has spent nearly a decade and a half shifting more than 200 tons of rocks in the hope of stalling the erosion of cliffs lining the north Norfolk coast.

JUNE: Postbox Snapper

Another Worcestershire man, Peter Willis has photographed more than 2,500 different postboxes. Just another 98,000 to go and he's got the lot.

JULY: Cone Ranger

Cotswold collector David Morgan has a houseful of traffic cones – more than 500 at the last count – including rarities washed up on European beaches and at least one which is nearly sixty years old. Rather than stealing them, he carries a supply of spares in the car and if he spots one he'd like he offers to swap it.

AUGUST: Busted

Roland Stone from Plymouth owns more than 500 scale models of double-deckers, but only proper ones, as he doesn't like hoppers or mini-buses. When his local newspaper ran a feature on him suggesting he was a bit odd, readers responded in his defence, while admitting to their own passions for collecting everything from Google logos through souvenir shoes from 1940s Hawaii to cheap plastic Christmas cracker toys.

SEPTEMBER: Brick-sure

Since being given his first brick in 1990, Neil Brittlebank from West Yorkshire spends his days scouring abandoned buildings and demolition sites and has so far built up a collection of more than a thousand different types.

OCTOBER: Greengrocers' Scourge

The founder of the Apostrophe Protection Society, Lincolnshire man John Richards is determined not to see the little chaps abused or abandoned.

NOVEMBER: Bladerunner

A retired greenkeeper, Stan Hardwick from Filey in Yorkshire has a pretty small garden – just 37 square metres – but a collection of more than 365 lawnmowers to keep it looking nice.

DECEMBER: Hedge Fun Manager

Hugh Barker has travelled the country photographing hedges. Unusual among members in that he doesn't wear a cardigan and is not yet retired, Barker has also published a book about his journeys entitled *Hedge Britannia: A Curious History of a British Obsession*.

THE MAN IN THE IRON MASK

In 1907, the fifth Earl of Lonsdale made a bizarre $100,000 bet with the American banker J. P. Morgan. The two millionaires were fortunate in finding a loser called Harry Bensley who agreed to undertake a near-circumnavigation of the globe on foot in order to settle the terms of their wager.

Bensley had been a successful businessman but by 1907 was down on his luck. He leapt at the opportunity to reverse his fortunes, agreeing to play the central role in the wager in return for which all his debts would be cancelled. Bensley thus undertook to visit 169 British towns and cities in a specified order, and another 125 in eighteen foreign countries, while satisfying various conditions along the way including:

Remaining incognito, by wearing a heavy iron mask from a suit of armour.

Collecting signatures in each city to prove that he had been there.

Financing the entire journey by selling postcards of himself.

Pushing a baby's perambulator the whole distance (containing the postcards and spare underclothes).

And finding himself a wife along the way, while still remaining incognito.

Bensley accordingly set off from London on New Year's Day 1908. He was quickly arrested, but it is not known whether this was for selling postcards without a hawker's licence, or for selling a postcard to Edward VII but then creating some confusion by refusing to sign it, as this would have given away his identity.

Such confusion is typical of the whole eccentric enterprise and in truth little is known of Bensley – for example, he was almost certainly married already – nor indeed of his adventures. By most accounts he completed much of the journey, and received (but rejected) approximately 200 proposals from women content to marry a man whose face they could not see and whose identity they could not know.

What is known is that by August 1914 he was in Genoa, northern Italy, claiming to have 30,000 miles under his belt and just seven countries left to go. Alas, the rapid escalation of what came to be known as the Great War made it impossible for him to continue, and possibly after being compensated by Lonsdale (Morgan had died the year before), he returned to England and may have enlisted. By the following year he had been invalided out, and after a succession of lowly paid jobs and a spell as a Labour councillor in Wivenhoe, Essex, he retired to a bedsit in Riley Road, Brighton. Despite detailed searches by his descendants, neither the mask nor the pram have been discovered.

15

Criminal England

'The incidence of crime has increased with the growth of the working-class population and there is more crime than in any other country in the world.'

Friedrich Engels (1820–95), co-father of Marxism,
during his time in Manchester

THE LAW IS AN ASS: TRUE OR FALSE?

'It is illegal to keep a lunatic without a licence.'

The Madhouses Act (1774) did indeed require anyone keeping 'more than one lunatick' to license the premises but this has since been repealed. ☞ FALSE.

■ ■ ■

'Members of Parliament may not enter the House of Commons wearing a suit of armour.'

This has been the case since 1313 and, as swords may not be taken into the Commons or Lords, coat-hooks in the Palace of Westminster have little ribbons or loops for suspending bladed weapons. ☞ TRUE.

■ ■ ■

'Putting a postage stamp upside down on an envelope is an act of treason.'

In 1848, the Treason Felony Act made it an offence to 'deprive or depose' the sovereign of the Imperial Crown, but no mention is made of her image on postage stamps. ☞ FALSE.

■ ■ ■

'It is illegal to impersonate a Chelsea Pensioner.'

From 1695 until 2008, regulations relating to all army pensions sensibly prevented anyone claiming any to which they weren't due. Simply donning a scarlet frock coat, however, is not an offence. ☞ FALSE.

■ ■ ■

'It is an offence to write on a fiver, but all right to light a cigar with it.'

Bizarrely, under the terms of the Currency and Banknotes Act 1928, it is illegal to deface a banknote but not to destroy one. It is, however, an offence to destroy a decimal coin, even if it's only a penny. ☞ TRUE.

■ ■ ■

'It is illegal to eat Christmas Pudding on Christmas Day.'

It was – Cromwell banned pretty much everything which made life enjoyable, and on Christmas Day 1644 refused to allow anyone to eat anything – but the restoration of Charles II also restored Christmas. ☞ FALSE.

■ ■ ■

'No one is allowed to die in the House of Commons.'

Unfortunately, no one told Sir Alfred Bilson this, who collapsed during a vote in 1907. The idea is that, as the Palace of Westminster is still a royal palace, someone dying on the premises is somehow entitled to a State Funeral. This is nonsense and he didn't get one. Nor did the prime minister Spencer Perceval after being shot dead in 1812, or indeed Guy Fawkes after his beheading. ☞ FALSE.

■ ■ ■

'It's illegal to fire a cannon at a house.'

Under Section 55 of the Metropolitan Police Act 1839, it is an offence to fire a cannon anywhere near a house. (The Act specified 300 yards or 274 metres.) ☞ TRUE.

■ ■ ■

'Englishmen are required to practise archery for two hours a week.'

The Unlawful Games Act (1541) demanded able-bodied men aged seventeen to sixty to keep a longbow and practise regularly. This is no longer the case, although incredibly the act wasn't repealed until 1960. ☞ FALSE.

■ ■ ■

'It is illegal to carry a plank along a pavement.'

Section 54 of the Metropolitan Police Act 1839 lists this as an offence, together with other annoyances such as flying kites in the street and sliding along icy pavements. ☞ TRUE.

'It is an offence to beat or shake a carpet in the street.'

Before 8 a.m. residents are permitted to beat or shake their doormats, but under Section 8 of the Town Police Clauses Act 1847 they are forbidden to beat or shake carpets. ☞ TRUE.

■ ■ ■

'It is illegal to keep a pigsty in your front garden or to kill a cow in the street.'

Both activities have been illegal since 1847 in towns and cities. It is also an offence to play knock-down ginger, run a washing line across the road, or to allow any of your servants to stand on a windowsill. ☞ TRUE.

■ ■ ■

'It is an offence to be drunk in charge of gun.'

Happily, this is correct. Inebriates should also avoid being found in possession of a horse, cow or steam engine, under the terms of the Licensing Act 1872. ☞ TRUE.

■ ■ ■

'It's illegal to be drunk in a pub.'

You can drink in a pub providing you're old enough, but being found drunk in one has been an offence for nearly a 150 years. Since 2003 it has also been illegal to buy a drink for a mate if you know he is drunk. ☞ TRUE.

■ ■ ■

'Welshmen in Chester can legally be shot dead after dark.'

A city ordinance dated 1403 reportedly imposed a curfew on Welshmen living in Chester – a reasonable response to Owain Glyndŵr's bid for independence – but murder is murder, and it has since been superseded by Article 2 of the European Convention on Human Rights. ☞ FALSE.

'A person with the plague can hail a cab but not catch a bus.'

A person with bubonic plague, rabies or leprosy is not allowed to travel on a bus, not even upstairs, but it is the driver who commits the offence by letting you board, so you'd be in the clear. Otherwise, the Public Health (Control of Disease) Act 1984 means you must warn a taxi driver in advance, but he's still allowed to take your money as long as he informs the local authority afterwards and cleans out his cab. ☞ TRUE.

■ ■ ■

'It's an offence to detonate an atomic weapon anywhere in England.'

The Nuclear Explosions Act (1998) was quite specific on this point, and to avoid any misunderstandings the then Home Secretary, Labour's Jack Straw, confirmed in writing that any person who knowingly causes such an explosion 'is guilty of an offence and liable on conviction on indictment to imprisonment for life'. ☞ TRUE.

ENGLAND'S BIGGEST HEISTS IN HISTORY

£350,000,000 – Greenwich, London

In 2000, thieves broke into a De Beers exhibition at the new Millennium Dome, intending to leave with the flawless 203.04 carat 'Millennium Star' diamond. The raid, had it come off, would have been England's largest by a substantial margin, but the gang had been under surveillance for several weeks following an anonymous tip off to the Metropolitan

Police. Armed with smoke bombs, sledgehammers, nail guns and a JCB digger, four men were arrested just 'twelve inches from payday', as one of them later recalled.

£53,000,000 – Tonbridge, Kent

Disguised as policemen, a gang kidnapped the family of a Securitas employee charged with disposing of used banknotes on behalf of the Bank of England. Told they would be harmed if he did not cooperate, the employee was taken to the company's depot and tied up with more than a dozen staff. The gang escaped with more than £50 million, around half of which has since been recovered.

£40,000,000 – Mayfair, London

One of the big names in jewellery, Graff Diamonds, was, by no means for the first time, hit badly when two men, smartly dressed and carrying guns, entered the Bond Street store in 2009. They left with more than forty pieces of jewellery and a sales assistant, although the latter was released very shortly afterwards.

£40,000,000 – Knightsbridge, London

In 1987 an Italian, Valerio Viccei, entered the premises of the Knightsbridge Safe Deposit Centre, apparently intent on opening an account. Once inside he and his associates drew their guns and cleaned out scores of boxes after hanging a 'Closed' sign in the window. Viccei fled the country and might have got away with it, but was arrested after returning to reclaim a Ferrari bought with the proceeds. Released from prison in 2000, he was shot by police in Italy.

£26,000 – Heathrow Airport, London

In 1983 a gang of six, aided by an insider, raided a warehouse near the airport, pouring petrol on staff and threatening to light a match. Expecting to rob a few million in currency, they escaped from the Brink's-MAT facility with more than 3 tonnes of gold bullion. Several gang members have since served time for this and other offences, but most of their haul was never recovered and around half is assumed to have been melted down and put back into circulation via legitimate channels.

£23,000,000 – Mayfair, London

In another strike against Graff in 2003, two Eastern Europeans armed with handguns removed forty-seven pieces of diamond jewellery in less than three minutes. Nicknamed the 'Pink Panthers', they are thought to be members of a group responsible for robbing more than one hundred shops in Monaco, the Middle East, Switzerland, Japan, France, Liechtenstein, Germany, Luxembourg and Spain.

£6,600,000 – Salford, Manchester

When a Securicor driver was forced to admit gang members to the secure Midland Bank Clearing Centre near Manchester, they escaped with £6.6 million in cash. This has never been recovered, nor have the perpetrators ever been identified. Instead, the van driver was convicted in 2002 and jailed for fourteen years, but after two years his conviction was quashed when it became apparent that he had cooperated with the robbers only under duress.

£6,000,000 – Shoreditch, London

On Easter Monday in 1983, a gang broke into the east London Security Express depot before escaping with around £6 million in cash. More than a decade later Ronnie Knight, married to *Carry On* actress Barbara Windsor for more than twenty years, confessed to having handled some of the cash. He was jailed for seven years and on his release, after admitting he was 'skint', the criminal mastermind moved into sheltered accommodation in Cambridge.

£3,000,000 – Baker Street, London

In 1971, a gang known as the 'Sewer Rats' spent days tunnelling into a vault beneath a branch of Lloyds Bank from the basement of Le Sac, a shop nearby selling leather goods. Four men were caught, charged, convicted and jailed but the case aroused little interest in Fleet Street, leading people to suppose that a D-Notice prevented editors from fully reporting on the proceedings. Since then, rumours have persisted about compromising documents being found in a safety deposit box, either one belonging to the Lord Chancellor Quintin Hogg or containing compromising photographs of a senior royal. These have not been substantiated.

£2,600,000 – Ledburn, Buckinghamshire

Magnets for morons, and inexplicably regarded as folk heroes by the same twerps who think the Krays were cool, in 1963 armed robbers stole sackloads of banknotes from a Glasgow-to-London Royal Mail train, after coshing the driver with an iron bar. Leaving fingerprints everywhere, and doing the worst possible job of lying low, all were quickly arrested and the following January received heavy sentences with ten of them sharing a total of 300 years.

NO WHINE, NO FEE

Whiplash claims and ambulance-chasing lawyers are a recent phenomenon, but there's nothing new about frivolous claims, as the following examples from the Norwich Union archives demonstrate all too well.

1878: A Lancashire grocer successfully claimed £15 after slipping over during a game of Blind Man's Buff.

1885: A chemist tripped on a set of marble steps at his local Turkish Baths and settled for £33.

1886: After being blown over by a gust of wind, an artist received £30 compensation.

1892: An Essex man received £50 after throwing rice at a wedding, only to have a grain blow back and lodge in his eye.

1895: Another man was injured jumping out of bed – in a bid, he said, to catch his wife who had fainted – and received £42 for his pains.

1900: A boatbuilder in Great Yarmouth in Norfolk was a £1,000 better off after swallowing a fishbone, and a bank clerk £156 richer after slipping on a piece of orange peel.

1904: After bumping his head whilst watching a tram accident from the top of another tram, a travelling salesman received £7.

16

Gruesome England

'There may be books out there reported to be covered in human skin which aren't, and others that are covered in skin but aren't known.'

Simon Chaplin, director of culture & society,
Wellcome Trust

The former head of London's superb Wellcome Library was reflecting on a time-honoured tradition, but one that probably won't be part of the recent revival in the craft of bookbinding. Chaplin was speaking after the discovery by staff at Harvard University of a book bound in skin, but actually there is no need to travel that far to find examples of this grisly practice: indeed, the Wellcome Library has one of its own.

Librarians call it anthropodermic bibliopegy, and there are several other examples in this country. The American volume, *Des Destinees de l'Ame* (The Destinies of the Soul) is thought to have been bound in the skin of a female mental patient in the 1880s, but in England the skin of executed criminals seems to have been the material of choice when this fashion was at its height.

Bristol's M Shed museum, for example, has a book about the trial of John Horwood, an eighteen-year-old who became the first man to be hanged at the city's New Gaol after battering a young woman to death in 1821. In the manner of the times, the murderer's corpse was dissected as part of a public lecture at Bristol's Royal Infirmary, after which the skin was stripped off and tanned.

The skin has mellowed to a dark coffee brown, and is decorated with embossed skulls and bones and the brief description in gold lettering: *Cutis Vera Johannis Horwood* ('Actual skin of John Horwood'). Almost as bizarre is the eventual fate of the body: in 2011, Horwood's skeleton was discovered hanging in a cupboard by his four-times great-niece, who arranged for a proper burial exactly 190 years after his execution.

Bury St Edmunds in Suffolk has a similar relic, a book bound in the skin of William Corder, who was convicted of killing Maria Marten in the pretty village of Polstead in 1828. What became known as the Red Barn Murder captivated newspaper readers at the time, and still fascinates visitors to Moyses Hall Museum with the book bound in his skin, his desiccated scalp, and a death mask. From the shape of Corder's skull, the dissecting surgeons concluded that his problems were due to excessive 'secretiveness, acquisitiveness, destructiveness, philoprogenitiveness, and imitativeness'. For years, his skeleton was on display at the nearby West Suffolk Hospital, where a mechanical device attached to one arm enabled it to lift and point to a charity box each time a visitor approached.

Like Horwood's, his book relates to the trial, but the third example is a book of poetry, making it even more bizarre.

The Poetical Works of John Milton belongs to the Westcountry Studies Library in Exeter and only came to light relatively recently, when it was donated by a member of the public.

This time, the skin is from a ratcatcher called George Cudmore. He was hanged in 1830 for murdering his wife Grace with a glass of milk laced with arsenic, apparently after forming an attachment to their lodger. Once again, his body was sent for dissection, after which the skin somehow fell into the hands of a local bookseller called Clifford. He must have held on to it for some years as the book is dated 1852, but no connection between himself and Cudmore has been discovered, nor indeed with John Milton.

BAKE, BOIL OR BURN

Besides its obvious curiosity value, the ghoulish practice of binding books using skin from convicted killers falls into the long tradition of ensuring the humiliation of the guilty continues as far beyond the grave as possible.

It's true that latterly attempts were made to devise a means of execution that was quicker and less painful than it had been – a sudden neck-snapping in place of slow strangulation – but for centuries the authorities inflicted as much ghastliness as possible before the accused was dispatched to the great courtroom in the sky. That people could be executed – and were – for such minor crimes as stealing a turnip, consorting with gypsies, or being out after dark with a sooty face only multiplies the horror.

Boiling

From 1531 to 1547, cooking someone to death was permitted under 'Statute 22', and 'William Boilman' joined the list of graphic nicknames by which executioners came to be known. The precise recipe is now lost to history, which is probably no bad thing, but poisoners William Roose in London and Margaret Davy in Kings Lynn are thought to have taken around two hours to die, which suggests the process began with the water, or oil, still cold.

Burning

The familiar image is of a witch or heretic, but burning was often employed against criminals too, particularly women accused of petty treason (killing their husbands) or of counterfeiting or clipping coins. It, too, was horribly slow: the calves, thighs and hands burning first, then the torso and forearms, finally the chest and face. So slow, indeed, that friends and family would sometimes seek to bribe the executioner to strangle their loved one beforehand or hang a pouch of gunpowder around her neck to ensure a quicker and more spectacular exit.

Beheading

The relative speed of decapitation explains why it was generally reserved for a privileged upper class, but even this didn't always go according to plan. The neck of Mary Queen of Scots took three attempts to sever, and in 1541 nearly a dozen blows were needed to finish off the sixty-seven-year-old Countess of Salisbury. This explains the consideration shown to Anne Boleyn by a merciful Henry VIII, who paid extra to have a French swordsman do the deed. The alternative would have been a drunk and incompetent Londoner, someone like Jack Ketch who, failing to do the job properly in 1685, pulled out a pocketknife to finish off the rebellious Duke of Monmouth.

Peine Forte et Dure

Until 1772, aristocrats could select this means of execution in which they were pressed to death beneath a door or board loaded up with heavy weights. French for 'hard and forceful punishment', it was as painful as it sounds and hideously prolonged. The sole upside was a legal loophole which allowed anyone choosing to exit this way to avoid having their property seized by the Crown. Choosing to be flattened instead of entering a plea of guilty or not guilty, a rich nobleman charged with a capital offence could thus ensure that, in return for his own suffering, his widow and heirs could inherit his estates.

Halifax Gibbet

Not everyone could afford a fancy French swordsman, and particularly up north where felons could be hanged for the theft of goods worth as little as 13½ old pence (6p), the authorities needed something more efficient than an axe and block. The Halifax Gibbet looked and worked just like a guillotine and was operational by the 1500s – which is to say, a couple of centuries at least before its more famous French counterpart. It remained in use until Oliver Cromwell called a halt in 1650, France once again lagging well behind the curve as it continued to guillotine its citizens until as recently as 1977.

Hanging, Drawing and Quartering

For centuries, the penalty for high treason was to be fastened to a hurdle or panel and drawn to the place of execution. The hanging caused only partial strangulation, and while still alive the individual would be disembowelled – possibly with the additional refinement of having his innards burnt before his eyes – and then beheaded and cut into quarters. The five portions would then be displayed around the country to discourage others from following his example (for the sake of public decency, female traitors were spared the punishment and burnt instead). In theory, the penalty remained available to the courts until 1870, although by the nineteenth century the beheading and quartering was usually delayed until the victim was actually dead.

Public Execution

In 1820, after plotting to kill the prime minister and cabinet, five of the Cato Street conspirators were the last men in England to be publicly beheaded. The last public hanging, however, took place in London as late as 1868, meaning that for several years it was possible to travel to a public execution by Tube, although such a day out was never suggested on any of London Underground's celebrated promotional posters. Executions after this date of course continued apace but then were out of sight of the public. Of the 763 such sentences carried out in England and Wales after 1900 – the last being Gwynne Evans and Peter Allen, two petty criminals who killed a man during a bungled break-in – a worryingly high proportion now appear to have been intentional miscarriages of justice.

Surprisingly, executions were never that common at the Tower of London, either. The busiest period was during World War I, when eleven German spies were shot – more than were beheaded in nearly a century and a half of Tudor rule – and the last to go was another German, Josef Jakobs, in August 1941.

THE ART OF PERSUASION

Among its advertised benefits Magna Carta made torture illegal in England after 1215, at least without a royal warrant. For a while no warrants were forthcoming until Edward II, leaned on by the pope, decided to permit the use of torture against the Knights Templar.

Inevitably there was a certain amount of mission creep here, and as more warrants were issued the practice spread. By the sixteenth century it was commonplace, and the devices used for the purpose increasingly ingenious.

The Collar

Among the possessions of Henry VIII was a heavy, lead-filled 'stele color for a prysonr', consisting of two iron semi-circles which lock together. The upper and lower edges of the collar have six pyramidal spikes extending from them, greatly increasing the discomfort of the wearer.

Ducking Stools

Usually reserved for prostitutes and witches, this involved a chair hung from the end of a pivoting arm. A woman could be swung out over a river, and dunked repeatedly. The process could be so prolonged as to last all day, and was still in use at Liverpool's Bridewell gaol at the end of the eighteenth century.

The Rack

To the sound of ligaments stretching and popping, victims would often be made to observe someone else being racked before they were themselves strapped into place. After being subjected to a lengthy spell in its deadly embrace, the Catholic martyr Edmund Campion admitted he didn't feel bad but only because he could no longer feel anything at all.

The Scavenger's Daughter

Devised during the reign of Henry VIII and named for Sir Leonard Skeffington, Lieutenant of the Tower of London, this was a metal A-frame to which the victim would be strapped. Besides the excruciating discomfort of contortion, blood would be forced from the nose and ears.

Thumbscrews

A primitive portable vice to crush fingers, thumbs and toes, the device often required a blacksmith to release the unfortunate digits. A similar contraption was sometimes used in an attempt to straighten the fingers of well-born Tudor girls – possibly even Princess Elizabeth herself.

ROOM 101

Established in 1874, the famous Black Museum in Room 101 at New Scotland Yard is soon to be opened to the public, displaying a grisly collection of crime-related artefacts confiscated under the auspices of the Prisoners Property Act (1869).

Exhibits include an authentic letter from Jack the Ripper, the gas stove and cooking pot used by serial killer Dennis Nilsen to boil the flesh of as many as fifteen victims in the 1970s and 1980s, and a leather apron worn by John Haigh, the acid bath killer, while dispatching his victims.

Among the collection of hangman's nooses are those used to hang Allen and Evans in 1964 (see above), and a row of death masks that provide a haunting reminder of those who entered Newgate Gaol in the City of London, but never came out alive.

Inevitably, weapons form a large part of the collection, including a crossbow belonging to a Kray associate, an IRA rocket launched at the MI6 building in 2006, even the microscopically small poisoned pellet which killed Bulgarian dissident Georgi Markov after he was stabbed with an umbrella whilst waiting for a bus in London. Most mysterious of all, perhaps, is a tomato ketchup bottle found at the Great Train Robbers' hideout at Leatherslade Farm near Oakley in Buckinghamshire – but only because after more than fifty years there's still no one at the Met. who will say why it's important.

The police insist that their Crime Museum (the term 'Black' was coined by an *Observer* journalist shortly after it opened) has a serious purpose, namely the study and detection of criminal behaviour.

17

Screening England

*'The British Film Industry: Elitist,
Deluded or Dormant?'*

Movie title, 2014

The Brisitsh film industry attracts hundreds of millions of pounds a year in tax, tax deals and lottery money, yet it employs less than 0.001 per cent of the population. And even now, more than thirty years after actor Colin Welland assured everyone at the Oscars that 'the British are coming!', it seems cruel to point out he was quoting an American revolutionary who was speaking at the start of a war we were never going to win.

A SLOW START FOR A GLOBAL PHENOMENON

- The first person to play James Bond was an actor called Barry Nelson, who appeared in a 1954 low-budget, black-and-white television special, for which author Ian Fleming was paid just £600.

- Two years later, *Blockbusters* quizmaster Bob Holness was offered the role – this time for another bargain-basement radio version – but for good or ill, no recording of this has survived.

- Carmaker Ford then briefly considered sponsoring a second made-for-television adventure (this time based on the book *From Russia with Love*, with James Mason as 007) but pulled out before shooting began.

- When finally the first big-screen version did appear, it featured the unknown Sean Connery behind the wheel of a puny 1.5-litre Sunbeam Alpine. This was because the owner of Aston Martin, tractor-magnate David Brown, wasn't happy about the idea of 007 driving one of his cars.

- At the time, 1962, American distributors were no more enthusiastic and bypassed the major cinemas completely. Instead, *Dr No* (1962) made its debut at an Oklahoma drive-in, and after seeing it for the first time Fleming commented tersely, 'Dreadful. Simply dreadful.'

HOLLYWOOD'S ENGLISH BIGSHOTS

❧ Cary Grant, real name Archie Leach, was born in Horfield, a suburb of Bristol. Aged nine, he was told his mother had died, but in his thirties discovered she had been placed in a lunatic asylum.

❧ Leslie Towns Hope, better known as Bob, was born in Eltham, south London, the son of a Welsh cleaner and a stonemason from Weston-super-Mare.

❧ Stan Laurel, born Arthur Stanley Jefferson, came from Ulverston in Cumbria, and attended grammar school in Bishop Auckland, Co. Durham.

❧ Bill Pratt was born in Honor Oak in south London. Before adopting the name Boris Karloff he dropped out of university, worked as a farmhand and eventually fell into acting.

❧ Angela Lansbury arrived in the US aged fourteen, having been born in London, the daughter of a communist mayor of Poplar, east London.

❧ Charlie Chaplin spent his childhood – 'a forlorn existence' – living in poverty in Lambeth, south London.

❧ James Stewart worked at Hull Repertory Theatre and Birmingham Rep. before changing his name to Stewart Granger, moving to Hollywood and taking American citizenship.

❧ Peter Mayhew, 'Chewbacca' in the *Star Wars* films, was born in Surrey and worked as a hospital orderly before getting the part. He studied animals at London Zoo in order to get his body language right.

- Mayhew's colleague, the Bristolian David Prowse, famously played the 1970s road-safety guru Green Cross Man ahead of his non-speaking role as 'Darth Vader'.

- *Sex and the City* star Kim Cattrall spent her formative years in Canada but was born in Mossley Hill, Liverpool.

AT HOME WITH 'AUNTY'

- In 1922 the BBC had only four employees, and a licence cost 10 shillings, or 50p. On first viewing John Logie Baird's invention, no one there found any 'excitement or interest' in the new technology, and a decision was taken to stick with radio.

- Television services nevertheless began at the end of 1936, but were suspended less than three years later with the outbreak of another war against Germany.

MORE OF THIS, PLEASE

On 18 April 1930, at 6.30 p.m. from a studio on London's Savoy Hill, an announcer for the BBC reported quite seriously that, as there was no news that day, listeners were invited to enjoy some piano music instead. So much better than just wittering on.

⋇ The Corporation began publishing the *Radio Times* in order to counteract Fleet Street, which for years refused to tell readers what was being broadcast for fear that they would start tuning in instead of buying a newspaper.

⋇ The first outside broadcast is generally held to be the coronation of George VI in 1937 but was actually a brief clip of comedian Leonard Henry climbing into his car outside Alexandra Palace the previous year.

⋇ In October 1940 a massive bomb fell on Broadcasting House killing seven. The blast could be heard on a live news bulletin but the newscaster Bruce Belfrage didn't even mention it for fear of breaching wartime security regulations.

⋇ By 1951 there were still only two transmitters in the entire country, and a very basic television with a tiny flickering screen cost about two months' wages for a labourer. This meant very few people could afford to buy one, although Queen Elizabeth II's coronation two years later provided a massive boost to sales.

⋇ At this time all broadcasts were black-and-white but the Beeb still recorded the events at Westminster Abbey in colour and even made a primitive version in 3D, which nobody had the technology to watch.

⋇ When ITV launched its rival service in 1955, the BBC ran a spoiler by controversially killing off 'Grace Archer' in a fire on its long-running radio soap.

⋇ In 1964 the Corporation suffered its own setback, when the launch of BBC Two was interrupted by a power cut which badly disrupted transmission on its opening night.

- In 1966 coverage of the football World Cup final had to be shared with ITV, but a total of 32.5 million viewers made it a record-breaking broadcast for the time.

- In 1967 colour televisions finally went on sale, with the first colour broadcasts coming from the minority channel BBC Two in July. Because the equipment at BBC One was too old-fashioned to broadcast anything except black-and-white, the first programme ever shown in colour was tennis from Wimbledon with David Vine.

TITFIELD TRIVIA: ENGLAND'S MUCH-LOVED EALING STUDIOS

The name of the *Titfield Thunderbolt* (1953) came from combining Titsey and Limpsfield, two villages near the Surrey home of scriptwriter T. E. B. Clarke.

■ ■ ■

Clarke's neighbour was the railway-rationalizing Richard Beeching who provided some of the dialogue for *The Man in the White Suit* (1951).

■ ■ ■

Nancy Mitford and Evelyn Waugh were both hired to write the script for *Kind Hearts and Coronets* (1949), although contributions from neither of them made it to the final cut.

Alec Guinness was originally contracted to play just four members of the d'Ascoyne family in the same film, but he liked the screenplay so much that he pestered the producers until they agreed to allow him to play all eight.

A special, less ambiguous ending had to be shot for

the American version of *Kind Hearts and Coronets* (1950), because US law at the time did not allow movies to suggest that crime might pay.

■ ■ ■

The same restriction required an announcement to be made at the end of *Whisky Galore* (1949), confirming that the stolen liquor brought nothing but unhappiness to the islanders.

As one of the stars of *Whisky Galore* Joan Greenwood was required to do some Scottish dancing. Despite, or as she insisted because of, her ballet training she was so bad at it that a local girl had to be hired for the close-up shots of her feet.

When a mock-up of the *Whisky Galore* ship sank before filming even began the studio saved itself some money by reusing footage of a different ship sinking from one of its wartime dramas, *San Demetrio London* (1943).

■ ■ ■

The outside scenes for *Passport to Pimlico* (1949) were actually shot on a bombsite on the opposite side of the River Thames in Lambeth.

■ ■ ■

For *The Lavender Hill Mob* (1951), the studio sought the help of the Bank of England in devising a way in which thieves could get away with stealing the then unheard-of sum of £1 million in gold bullion.

■ ■ ■

Mrs Wilberforce's pet birds in *The Ladykillers* (1955) were voiced by Peter Sellers, who cheekily has a parrot say 'Alec Guinness' at one point in the film.

In the same film, a taxicab driven by the slow-witted boxer 'One-Round' Lawson is an Austin at the beginning of the journey but changes to a Morris halfway along before reverting to an Austin again.

■ ■ ■

James Robertson Justice appeared in *The Magnet* (1950), but insisted on a Gaelic pseudonym in the credits as he was hoping to stand for Parliament as a Labour candidate. He did so, and lost.

■ ■ ■

Meet Mr Lucifer (1953) was based on a play by Arnold Ridley, who subsequently played 'Private Godfrey' in television sitcom *Dad's Army* (1968–77).

CINEMA'S GOLDEN AGE

England's First Cinema

- On 21 March 1896, England's first picture house opened at the junction of London's Shaftesbury Avenue and Piccadilly Circus. Birt Acres showed several silent shorts, including *The Arrest of a Pickpocket* and *The Comic Shoeblack*, before his Kineopticon was razed to the ground in a fire.

- The Odeon cinema chain insists the name is short for 'Oscar Deutsch Entertains Our Nation' but the term was already in use in France before 1928 when Deutsch opened his first cinema in Brierley Hill near Birmingham.

The J. Arthur Rank Organization

The eponymous founder, a devout Methodist and Sunday School teacher, started out making low-budget religious films.

J. Arthur's father always considered his son to be a bit of a dunce, but after taking over the family flour-milling business the younger man transformed it into Rank-Hovis-MacDougall, a FTSE-100 conglomerate which was later sold for more than £1 billion.

The gong at the start of all Rank films is actually made from cardboard, the sound recorded separately from a much smaller tam-tam.

The Gaumont State Cinema, Kilburn

This London cinema boasts a central tower modelled on the Empire State Building. At 37 metres, it is less than a twelfth of the height of the New York original, but with a capacity of 4,004, in 1937 the auditorium was, by some margin, England's largest.

The Blue Walnut Café, Chelston

Today, the smallest cinema is found in Torquay, seating just twenty-three.

The Curzon, Clevedon

Somerset claims the longest continuously used, purpose-built cinema in the world. Indeed, it's so old that when it first opened it appealed for funds to help survivors of the RSS *Titanic*, which had just been lost at sea.

18

Eating England

'To eat well in England, you should have breakfast three times a day.'

W. Somerset Maugham (1874–1965), author

Nicknamed the Banksy of breakfasts, mystery still surrounds the identity of the Fry-Up Inspector, an anonymous blogger who travels the country in search of the perfect English breakfast.

Having visited more than 300 establishments in London, Northampton, Cambridge, Brighton and Bristol – ranging from greasy spoons to farmshops and tea rooms – the inspector's reviews are now so widely read that establishments have begun putting stickers in their windows to advertise that they have received a visit. It's a cushy job and a proper cooked breakfast is hard to beat, but for all the bad press, England's contribution to world cuisine is greater than the critics would have you believe.

Afternoon Tea

If anything can be more English than a 'full English' then it's afternoon tea, which became something of a national institution after being dreamt up by Anna Russell, wife of the seventh Duke of Bedford. In 1840, feeling the need for something between luncheon and dinner, she began inviting friends to join her for Darjeeling and a light meal, and where duchesses go, others follow.

Balti

Served sizzling pretty much everywhere in the country, Balti is popularly supposed to have originated in Baltistan (in northern Pakistan), but was probably first eaten in Birmingham in the mid-1970s.

Bangers

With the English traditionally serving the crummiest sausages anywhere outside the Eastern bloc, the word 'banger' was coined shortly after the Great War to describe the way in which the cheapest possible ingredients would explode during the cooking process. Despite marked improvements in quality over the last twenty years, the name has stuck.

Bedfordshire Clanger

Described by novelist H. E. Bates as 'hard as a hog's back, harder 'n prison bread' this traditional lunchtime snack for fieldworkers has made a bit of a comeback in recent years. Essentially it's a suet pudding, with a savoury filling at one end and a sweet filling at the other. A complete meal in one sitting, it can be eaten while one hand remains on a tractor's steering wheel.

Bubble and Squeak

Also cockney rhyming slang for Greek, the earliest known recipe for the shallow-fried cabbage and potato leftovers appeared in 1806 in an English cookery book. The first edition of *A New System of Domestic Cookery* identified the author only as 'A Lady', but later reprints credited Mrs Maria Eliza Ketelby Rundell.

Champagne

Everyone knows the story of the French monk Dom Perignon and his celebrated wine-making rules. These were published in 1718 but an Englishman beat him to it, and by several decades. Christopher Merrett's 1662 paper, *Some Observations concerning the Ordering of Wines*, described the so-called 'méthode champenoise' of deliberately encouraging a secondary fermentation to produce sparkling bubbles in wine. (An average of 250 million of them per bottle, according to France's *Industrie et Technolgie de la Machine*.)

Cheddar Cheese

Henry II was consuming huge quantities of cheese from Somerset in 1170, with recipes that may have been brought from France by the Romans. However, the semi-hard cheese we know today is the creation of Joseph Harding. In the 1850s, he introduced new techniques and practices to produce the standardized product that Englishmen continue to love. It still accounts for just over half of the country's nearly £2 billion annual cheese expenditure.

Chine

Taking its name from the bony part of a chop rather than the geological feature, this is a Lincolnshire speciality of stuffed, brine-soaked pork. It is usually made with parsley, but after tasting one filled with leeks, spring onions, lettuce and raspberry leaves, the nineteenth-century poet Paul Verlaine (a schoolmaster in Boston at the time) spent weeks trying to track down other varieties around England, but found none.

Cornish Pasty

People seeking Cornish independence like to point to a recipe dated 1745 in the Records Office in Truro, and of course a new Protected Geographical Indication status means it's now illegal to make the tin-miner's favourite anywhere in the EU but Cornwall. However, the word comes from the medieval French *paste*, or pie, and a document proves they were being made in Norfolk in the thirteenth century, while numerous old photographs disprove the popular notion that the characteristic pasty ridge provided a 'handle' for grubby miners, which could then be discarded at the conclusion of the meal. Sorry Cornwall, but at least they're English so let's be grateful for that.

Cottage Pie

Frequently confused with the nineteenth-century shepherd's pie (containing lamb), the earliest known reference to the proper item dates back to 1791. Potatoes were cheap at this time but beef certainly wasn't, so it seems likely that the early versions included rather more 'thatch' than most modern consumers would consider good value.

Eccles Cake

Many northern towns claim to have something similar (as indeed does Banbury in the Midlands), but from his shop on the corner of Vicarage Road and Church Street in Eccles, James Birch was selling flaky pastry cakes stuffed with currants as early as 1793. It has yet to secure its own Protected Geographical Indication status but the Eccles is thought to be the only cake to carry an official warning from the Lancashire Fire & Rescue Service. In May 2013 the *Daily Mail* informed readers that its high sugar content had led to a rise in house fires following attempts to reheat shop-bought cakes in domestic microwave ovens.

Fish and Chips

After much debate and deliberation, the National Federation of Fish Friers recently published an official adjudication crediting Joseph Malin with the invention of this country's national dish. A Jewish immigrant from Eastern Europe, Malin was the first to combine traditional Jewish fried fish with the newly fashionable chipped potato. This was 1860, and he sold it from a shop in east London.

Fizzy Water

Clearly here to stay, bottled water was a largely continental habit until the 1980s, and one that most thought risible. Carbonated water was nevertheless an English invention, first offered to guests of Joseph Priestley in Birmingham in 1767. The gas which he called 'fixed air' killed mice, but also gave water a pleasant taste. As it was believed to have health-giving properties the term 'soda water' was adopted around 1799.

Haggis

First described in rhyme around 1430 in the *Liber Cure Cocorum* – a book of the cook's arts – 'hagese', a Lancashire combination of offal and herbs, has since been adopted as a national dish by our friends north of the border.

TO-MARROW, TO-MARROW, I LOVE YA, TO-MARROW

Lovingly nurtured by Ken Dade from Norfolk, at 65 kg the world's largest marrow needed two men to carry it into the marquee at the National Amateur Gardening Show at Shepton Mallet in Somerset. (Visitors to the event were also treated to the world's longest cucumber when Alf Cobb broke his own record with a 0.9-metre whopper.)

HP Sauce

Depressingly, the definitive brown sauce is now made in the Netherlands, but was devised by Nottingham grocer Frederick Garton in the 1890s. He chose the name in the belief that it was being served in the Houses of Parliament, but money worries meant Garton quickly had to sell rights to the recipe for just £150.

Jellied Eels

It says much for the eel that it was most plentiful when London's water was at its filthiest and most poisonous. Englishmen and eels have a long shared history, however, and the remains of several sixth- and seventh-century eel traps can still be seen at low tide in the Thames. As a cheap source of protein, Londoners used to love them, though once jellied they are very much the Marmite of the fish world. Chopped then boiled in vinegary water and cooled to jelly, presumably they travel badly, as no one has copied the cockney example.

Kendal Mint Cake

Popular among fellwalkers and mountaineers for its high energy content, the first mint cake was probably produced by accident in 1869 when a batch of confectionery went wrong and solidified overnight into a hard white mass. Included in the rations for Shackleton's Antarctic expedition of 1914 and Hillary and Tenzing's Everest conquest of 1953, mint cake is still made in the famous Lakeland town.

Lancashire Hotpot

Preferably using mutton, and including oysters until these were no longer plentiful or cheap, this meal was originally stewed in a tall brown earthenware pot over a low flame, while the family was out at work. Slow cooking meant cheap cuts worked best, but after a 150 years Lancastrians are still arguing over what constitutes the definitive recipe.

Lasagne

As 'loseyn', meaning lozenges, this was a popular dish during the unhappy reign of Richard II (1367–1400), and made its first appearance in an English cookbook, *Forme of Cury*. Thin, dried sheets of paste were cooked in broth, when tomatoes were unknown to both English and Italian cooks.

Parkin

This soft cake of flour, oatmeal, lard and black treacle originated in Leeds during the Industrial Revolution and is frequently eaten around Bonfire Night. Recent additions have included brandy and ginger, both unknown to nineteenth-century Yorkshire labourers.

Parmo

Peculiar to Middlesbrough, and served with chips, the parmo is a large chicken escalope deep fried in breadcrumbs, then covered with béchamel sauce, melted cheddar, pepperoni, bacon and garlic sauce.

Piccalilli

An Edwardian mainstay of picnics and cold collations, a reference in 1758 by cookery writer Hannah Glasse to 'Paco-Lilla, or India Pickle' suggests its origins lie with the Empire, although presumably the addition of marrow and cauliflower came later.

Port

It may hail from Portugal but so much wine from the Alto Douro region was exported to England that for more than 350 years even the Portuguese called it Englishman's Wine. Even now, at least half the producers are English, with firms such as Warre (founded in 1670), Croft (1678), Taylor, Fladgate & Yeatman, Sandeman, Cockburn and Graham dominating the market.

Sandwich

Combinations of meat or fish and bread have been enjoyed for millennia, but the snack which the *Wall Street Journal* insists is this country's single greatest contribution to gastronomy was first served to John Montagu, fourth Earl of Sandwich in the 1740s. Lord Sandwich wanted something he could eat with one hand, but whether this was so that he could carry on working on his ministerial papers or continue gambling has never been determined.

Scotch Egg

Inspired by a traditional Indian dish comprising a boiled egg served in a shell of ground lamb, the first of these was sold by a London grocer in 1738. A recipe to make them at home was included in a later edition of Mrs Rundell's English cookbook in 1809 (see 'Bubble and Squeak' on page 182) and the Scottish connection has never been explained. If the egg element is pickled then wrapped in black pudding it is known as a Manchester Egg.

Spotted Dick

Incredibly, Spotted Dick is not English, having made its first appearance in 1849's *The Modern Housewife or Ménagère*, by Frenchman Alexis Soyer. At least he lived in London, where as the greatest chef of his day he was employed by the Reform Club in London at a salary equivalent to nearly £3 million a year.

Worcestershire Sauce

Another happy accident, Lea & Perrins' fortune was built on the failure of its founders to recreate for a customer a sauce he had enjoyed whilst serving in India. Finding it too strong to consume, a barrel of the stuff was abandoned in the shop cellar. After several years, it was found to have mellowed, and in 1838 the first bottles were offered for sale. To the disappointment of many vegetarians, its mystery ingredient is anchovies.

Yorkshire Pudding

The earliest known recipe for the popular combination of eggs, flour and milk appeared in 1737, when it was still possible to get away with titles such as *The Whole Duty of a Woman, or An Infallible Guide to the Fair Sex*. At the time it was used to make pigeon-in-the-hole, which is exactly what it sounds like. Toad-in-the-hole arrived much later (1891), and bizarrely made its debut in an Italian recipe book rather than one of ours.

ODD PUBS TO PONDER OVER A PINT

The Black Castle, Brislington

As much as 250 years ahead of its time, Bristol's aptly named establishment could claim to be the first ever fully sustainable eco-pub. It was built in the 1760s by a copper smelter called William Reeve. Instead of bricks, he used spelter slag, a purplish-black by-product of the smelting process, which he cunningly recycled.

The Hatchet Inn, Bristol

This pub was built in Bristol in 1606. Beneath layers of paint and tar, the door is rumoured to be covered with human skin, although no one seems to know whose, or how it came to be there.

The Valiant Soldier, Buckfastleigh

This pub closed in the 1960s, since when everything – bottles, glasses, optics, the furniture and even the bills on the bar – has remained untouched.

The Lord Nelson, Burnham Thorpe

This Norfolk pub serves spiced brandy to commemorate local-boy-made-good, Viscount Nelson. When he was killed at Trafalgar, the admiral's body was preserved in a barrel of brandy for the voyage home, which his crew then drank in an attempt to imbibe the spirit of their great commander, or maybe just to drown their sorrows.

The Nutshell, Bury St Edmunds

This is one of several pubs to boast of being the smallest in the country. In 1984, a record 102 people squeezed in, occupying a corner plot no more than 7 or 8 feet deep, but even with only ten drinkers, it can feel almost too friendly.

White Hart, Canterbury

The only pub in England with a chute for dead bodies in the cellar, this was built on the ruins of an old church which had a mortuary in the undercroft.

The Nobody Inn, Doddiscombleigh

The Devon pub with the best name ever.

Well House, Exeter

This pub gets its name from an old well in the cellar, which is possibly Roman. Visitors can also see a collection of bones, believed to be those of a priest or monk and his girlfriend. Recognizing the impossibility of their love for each other, they are popularly supposed to have killed themselves by jumping down the well.

The Crooked House, Himley

Strictly speaking the Glynne Arms, although no one's used that name for this Staffordshire pub since Victorian mineworkings underneath threatened its collapse. Its doors and windows are all at odd angles and glasses slide across tables, but after massive underpinning by the local brewery, drinkers are assured it is entirely safe.

The Farmhouse, Kesgrave

Probably the only pub in England where one can quench a spiritual, as well as a physical, thirst, this pub near Ipswich regularly hosts church services in the bar.

The Sun, Leintwardine

Here, there are no bar staff. Customers serve themselves in one of the last remaining parlour pubs in the country, effectively just a licensed room in the licensee's house.

Ye Olde Trip to Jerusalem, Nottingham

England's oldest pub is built into the sandstone cliffs beneath Nottingham Castle, where its original brewhouse once stood. Clearly Norman, its name is a reference to the crusader Richard I's departure for the Holy Land in 1189.

Warren House, Postbridge

Drinkers are assured of the warmest welcome at this Devonshire pub, not least because the fire which was lit in 1845 has never been allowed to go out.

Fitzpatrick's, Rawtenstall

The country's only surviving teetotal pub, in Lancashire, opened its doors in 1832, when the temperance movement still hoped to turn young men away from the demon drink. Now, as then, customers can enjoy cream sodas, ginger cordial or Blood Tonic, brewed from raspberry, rosehip and nettle.

The Tan Hill, Reese

From the smallest to the highest, this pub in the Yorkshire Dales is 1,732 ft above sea level. It's a lonely but lovely spot.

The Haunch of Venison, Salisbury

Not for the first time, in 2010 a mummified hand was stolen from this pub in Salisbury. The grisly relic is thought to have been severed from the arm of a regular when a game of cards got out of . . . er, hand.

It hardly needs saying that any one of these old pubs would provide the perfect place to reflect on the wealth and variety of strange stuff this small country has to offer. So much of it that a single book can never do more than scratch the surface, and so much that anyone scratching away will quickly come to understand why Englishmen like to quote the Roman Horace: *Hic amor, haec patria est*. It is my love, it is my country.